621 SUPER WEIRD FACTS

TO BOGGLE YOUR BRAIN

ARCTURUS

This edition published in 2025 by Arcturus Publishing Limited
26/27 Bickels Yard, 151–153 Bermondsey Street,
London SE1 3HA

Copyright © Arcturus Holdings Limited

All rights reserved. No part of this publication may be reproduced, stored in a retrieval system, or transmitted, in any form or by any means, electronic, mechanical, photocopying, recording, or otherwise, without prior written permission in accordance with the provisions of the Copyright Act 1956 (as amended). Any person or persons who do any unauthorized act in relation to this publication may be liable to criminal prosecution and civil claims for damages.

Illustrator: Luke Séguin-Magee
Authors: Anne Rooney, Marc Powell, William Potter, Ben Hubbard,
  Clare Hibbert, Adam Phillips, and Helen Otway
Designer and Editor: Lucy Doncaster
Design Manager: Rosie Bellwood-Moyler
Managing Editor: Joe Harris

ISBN: 978-1-3988-5057-6
CH012479NT
Supplier 29, Date 0225, PI 00010031

Printed in China

CONTENTS

INTRODUCTION	4
BIZARRE BODIES	6
CHEW ON THIS	22
AWESOME ANIMALS	44
WATERY WORLD	58
PAST PECULIAR	74
SHOCKING SCIENCE	92
DARING DEEDS	110
FABULOUS FACTS	124
FREAKY FEATS	138
KOOKY SPORTS	154
PREPOSTEROUS PASTIMES	166

WELCOME ...

... to the fascinating world of the weird and wonderful. Within these pages, you'll discover 621 of the most astonishing, most intriguing, and most flummoxing facts you could possibly imagine. Covering everything from science to sports, hobbies to history, animals to appetites, and everything in between, there's something for everyone in this treasure trove of trivia tidbits.

Find out whether hot or cold water freezes faster, what happens in a chess boxing championship, which creature has a hundred eyes, where you can win a prize for making fart noises with your armpit, who can eat the most hotdogs in 10 minutes, and much, much more.

So what are you waiting for? It's time to turn the page and dive right in.

Bizarre Bodies

HOW FAST DO YOU REMEMBER?
Retrieving a memory takes 0.0004 seconds.

WHAT MAKES HAIR CURLY?
Whether your hair is curly or straight depends on the shape of your hair follicles. Curly hair grows from oval follicles, and straight hair grows from round follicles.

HOW MANY CELLS ARE IN YOUR BODY?
The average human body is made up of an astonishing 50 trillion cells.

HOW FAR DO BLOOD CELLS TRAVEL?
Red blood cells are made inside your bones. Each cell travels around the body about 250,000 times before it returns to the bone marrow to die.

Bizarre Bodies

DID YOU KNOW?
A Michigan couple opened a package delivered to their home and were shocked to find a liver and an ear inside! The parts should have been delivered to a nearby research laboratory.

DO LEFTIES AND RIGHTIES EAT DIFFERENTLY?
If you're right-handed, you tend to chew food on the right side of your mouth. If you're left-handed, you tend to chew on the left.

DID YOU KNOW?
You have no control over some of your muscles! These are known as involuntary muscles. The body uses them for functions such as breathing and digesting food.

ARE ADULTS' BRAINS BIGGER THAN KIDS'?
Yes—but not much! Your brain reached 90 percent of its adult size by the time you were six years old.

Bizarre Bodies

WHAT IS THE TOUGHEST THING IN YOUR BODY?
Tooth enamel is the hardest substance in your body.

DID YOU KNOW?
A British woman who lost her false teeth discovered that her dog had eaten them! The dog had a three-hour operation to have them removed.

WHAT IS ASPIRIN MADE OF?
The painkilling drug aspirin comes from willow bark. It was first described by a Greek philosopher named Hippocrates in the 5th century BCE.

WHAT PART OF YOUR BODY IS THE GREEDIEST?
Your brain is your hungriest organ! About 20 percent of the calories you eat feeds it.

Bizarre Bodies

CAN YOU TASTE WITH YOUR NOSE?
Your nose helps you taste things! That's why it's difficult to taste your food if you have a cold and can't smell anything.

HOW MUCH FOOD DO YOU EAT IN A LIFETIME?
Your digestive system will process around 50 metric tons (55 tons) of food in your lifetime.

WHAT'S A CRAMP?
Sometimes a muscle fully contracts by itself when you're not expecting it, and it is very painful—that's cramp!

DID YOU KNOW?
One person in 200 has an extra pair of ribs.

Bizarre Bodies

DOES RUBBING REDUCE PAIN?
Pain signals reach the brain more slowly than touch signals, so if you rub a sore area, then your brain recognizes that signal first.

DID YOU KNOW?
Your eyes always close when you sneeze—it is impossible to keep them open.

DID YOU KNOW?
In an emergency, your body will produce a hormone called adrenaline, which gives you incredible strength.

DO ALL ANIMALS CRY?
No. Humans are the only animals that cry tears when we are upset or hurt.

WHO OWNS A MUSEUM OF HAIR?
Wreaths, pictures, jewels, and postcards that are made of or contain human hair are on display in Leila's Hair Museum, in Missouri, USA. These keepsakes were commonly made in Victorian times.

Bizarre Bodies

DID YOU KNOW?
There are more than 700 kinds of bacteria lurking in your large intestine.

HOW LONG DO EYEBROWS LAST?
An eyebrow hair lasts for only 10 weeks, whereas a hair can stay on your head for about five years.

WHAT DOES YOUR HAIR SAY ABOUT YOU?
Forensic scientists can identify a person's age, sex, race, and state of health from a single hair.

WHO DIDN'T WASH HIS HAIR FOR DECADES?
An 80-year-old Chinese man agreed to have his hair washed for the first time in 23 years. It took 12 relatives and friends five hours to get all the grime out of his 2 m (6 ft)-long matted locks, followed by his beard, which measured 1.5 m (5 ft)!

Bizarre Bodies

HOW FAST CAN YOUR MUSCLES REACT?
Some of your muscles can contract and relax again in a fraction of a second, such as those in your eyes.

DID YOU KNOW?
You have more than 230 joints in your body.

WHAT'S SALIVA GOOD FOR?
Salivating before vomiting is the body's way of protecting your teeth from the high acid levels in vomit.

HOW HARD IS IT TO TALK?
You use 72 muscles when you talk. That's quite a workout!

DID YOU KNOW?
Earwax is a mixture of a type of sweat, dead skin cells, and an oily substance called sebum.

Bizarre Bodies

WHAT'S YOUR BODY'S BIGGEST INTERNAL ORGAN?
The liver is your largest internal organ—it has more than 500 functions and two blood supplies.

HOW DO PEOPLE MEASURE POOP?
There are seven types of poop listed on the Bristol Stool Chart medical aid, ranging from "separate hard lumps, like nuts" (Type 1) to "entirely liquid" (Type 7).

DID YOU KNOW?
It is possible to live without your large intestine.

HOW MANY TIMES DOES YOUR HEART BEAT?
Your heart beats more than 30 million times each year!

Bizarre Bodies

HOW MANY HAIRS DO YOU HAVE?

You are hairy all over! Only your lips, palms, and the soles of your feet have no hair on them—the rest of your body is covered in around 5 million hairs.

DID YOU KNOW?

The fingerprints of koalas and humans are so similar that they could be confused at a crime scene.

DID YOU KNOW?

Ears, eyes, and even bladders can all be replaced with machines.

HOW MANY TYPES OF EARWAX ARE THERE?

Two. The majority of people have wet ear wax, and a smaller proportion have dry ear wax. Which type you have depends on a single gene.

Bizarre Bodies

WHAT'S THE MOST DANGEROUS TIME OF DAY?
The human body is at its lowest ebb between 3 a.m. and 4 a.m. This is the most likely time for someone to die in their sleep.

CAN PEOPLE USE SONAR?
Yes! Some blind people have learned to click their tongues and listen for echoes as a way of detecting objects around them.

DID YOU KNOW?
The only animals that can get sunburned apart from humans are pigs, elephants, and rhinos.

WHERE IS THERE A HAMMER IN YOUR HEAD?
You have a stirrup, an anvil, and a hammer in each ear! They are tiny bones that were named at a time when there were more blacksmiths around than there are today.

Bizarre Bodies

DID YOU KNOW?
American toothpaste boxes from 1968 were black and featured an X-ray picture of a decayed tooth. Marketing has improved a little since then!

WHERE IS THE LONGEST BONE IN YOUR BODY?
Your thigh bone or femur is the longest bone in your body.

HOW FAST DO YOU FEEL?
Nerve signals are superfast! It takes less than one-hundredth of a second for a nerve signal from your toe to travel up to your brain.

IS LAUGHING DANGEROUS?
Laughing and coughing put more pressure on your spine than standing or walking do. Some people have even developed back injuries from coughing.

Bizarre Bodies

WHERE ARE YOUR BODY'S BIGGEST MUSCLES?
Your largest muscles are the ones you sit on! You have a gluteus maximus in each buttock.

DID YOU KNOW?
When reading, people typically blink only three times a minute.

WHICH MUSCLE NEVER GETS TIRED?
The only muscle in your body that never gets tired is your heart.

DO YOU GROW AT NIGHT?
The hormone that makes you grow is produced only when you sleep, so if you want to be taller, you should go to bed early!

DID YOU KNOW?
You could live for a month without food, but only for a week without water.

Bizarre Bodies

CAN YOU THICKEN YOUR FINGERNAILS?
Your nails are naturally thick or thin—nothing can make them thicker, whatever the claims on nail cosmetics may say!

HOW MANY MESSAGES CAN YOU MANAGE?
Each nerve cell in your brain can receive over 100,000 messages per second!

DID YOU KNOW?
A Yemeni man was found to have four kidneys instead of two. Although he was offered money for his spare ones, he decided that they were a gift from Allah and kept all four.

WHERE ARE SNEEZES APPROVED OF?
The ancient Greeks believed that a sneeze was a good sign from the gods.

Bizarre Bodies

DO WE HAVE TAILS?

Humans have a tailbone! Its proper name is the coccyx, which means cuckoo—it got its name because it looks like a cuckoo's beak.

DID YOU KNOW?

Your lungs are different sizes! The left one is smaller to make room for your heart.

HOW MUCH SKIN DO WE SHED?

We shed about 30,000 skin cells every minute! That amounts to about 5 billion skin cells each and every day.

HOW WET ARE YOU?

Your body is made up of 66 percent water.

Bizarre Bodies

HOW LONG CAN FINGERNAILS GROW?

An Indian man went 66 years without cutting his nails! They grew to a jaw-dropping 909.6 cm (358 in) before he finally gave them a trim in 2018.

DID HUMANS USED TO HAVE AN EXTRA EYELID?

Ever wondered what that little pink lump in the corner of your eye is? Our ancestors had an extra eyelid that would close horizontally to protect the eye. We haven't needed it for millions of years, so it has disappeared through evolution.

DID YOU KNOW?

Your ears get bigger as you age! This is due to the effects of gravity, not because they keep growing—which is a common myth.

WHAT HAPPENS IF YOU LOSE YOUR BRAIN CELLS?

Your brain's nerve cells, called neurons, are the only cells in the body that do not regenerate. When they're gone, they're gone!

CHEW ON THIS

Chew On This

DID YOU KNOW?
A New York restaurant offers the ultimate luxury pizza, topped with gold leaf, caviar, truffles, and foie gras. It's a bargain at more than $2,000!

WHY IS BUBBLEGUM PINK?
Early bubblegum was pink because it was the only food dye available at the time.

HOW DID THE TURPENTINE MANGO GET ITS NAME?
The turpentine mango smells of ... turpentine! It is safe to eat, but the experience is said to be like eating a regular mango in a freshly painted room.

WHERE SHOULD YOU GO TO FEAST ON RODENTS?
Mice are a delicacy in Zambia and Malawi.

Chew On This

WHOSE HOUSE IS THE CHEESIEST?
Canadian sculptor Cosimo Cavallaro sprayed a whole house with ... cheese! He used 4,534 kg (10,000 lb) of pepperjack to cover the house inside and out.

WHY WERE SAUSAGES INVENTED?
Sausages were invented thousands of years ago as a way of preserving and eating all the nasty-looking leftovers from slicing up an animal into cuts of meat.

HOW MANY EGGS DO CHICKENS LAY?
A chicken can lay more than 200 eggs a year.

WHAT'S THE USE OF PEANUTS?
American scientist George W. Carver invented over 300 products made from peanuts, including cloth dyes and wood stains.

Chew On This

WHO IS THE WORLD'S BIGGEST BAKED BEAN FAN?

Welshman Captain Beany worships baked beans! He dresses in baked bean orange, bathes in beans, and formed the New Millennium Bean Party.

WHO ATE THE ANIMAL KINGDOM?

Nineteenth-century English geologist William Buckland claimed to have eaten his way through the animal kingdom, including panther and crocodile. He said the worst things he had tasted were mole and bluebottle fly.

DID YOU KNOW?

China is the world's leading producer of apples.

DO PEOPLE EAT KANGAROOS?

Kangaroo meat is very low in fat—kangaroo sausages, known as kanga bangas, and kangaroo steaks are both available in Australia.

Chew On This

DID YOU KNOW?
Vinegar eels are tiny worms that can be found in vinegar. Don't worry—bottled vinegar is pasteurized and filtered, so you won't find any wriggling around in your salad dressing!

WHAT IS WITCHES'-BROOM FUNGUS?
Witches'-broom fungus and frosty pod rot are fungi that affect cacao plants —the plants used to make chocolate.

DID YOU KNOW?
Japanese artist Tatsumi Orimoto goes around the world's cities and shakes hands with people ... with baguettes strapped to his head, covering his face! He calls his performance art Bread Man.

WHERE CAN YOU EAT AN EGGS-TRA HUGE MEAL?
At Abbeville, Louisiana's Giant Omelette Celebration, 5,000 eggs are mixed together and cooked in a giant pan.

Chew On This

CAN YOU HATCH STORE-BOUGHT EGGS?
Sometimes, yes. A British girl put two store-bought organic eggs in an incubator to see if they would hatch. A few weeks later, two fluffy chicks popped out!

ARE TURKEYS FROM TURKEY?
Turkeys originally came from Mexico. Their English name comes from the fact that they were first brought to England from Turkey.

DID YOU KNOW?
Dried peas have been found in ancient Egyptian tombs.

WHAT CAME FIRST, POPCORN OR MOVIES?
Popcorn was discovered thousands of years ago by Native Americans, who enjoyed popcorn soup and popcorn beer. That's thousands of years before movies were invented!

Chew On This

CAN YOU MAKE PINEAPPLE JELLY?
No. Fresh pineapple contains an enzyme that prevents it from setting.

DID YOU KNOW?
The poisonous plant hemlock has a large white root and can be mistaken for wild parsnip ... with disastrous results!

DO WATERMELONS COME FROM A WET COUNTRY?
No, it's really the opposite! Watermelons grow wild in the Kalahari Desert.

DOES GARLIC HAVE ANY USES OTHER THAN KEEPING VAMPIRES AT BAY?
Garlic has long been used for its medicinal properties and was an ancient Egyptian cure for worms.

DID YOU KNOW?
Fortune cookies were actually invented in California, USA.

Chew On This

WHAT FOOD CAUSES THE MOST ALLERGIES?
More people are allergic to cows' milk than any other food.

DID YOU KNOW?
Dozens of people from northern India became seriously unwell in 1998 after using what they thought was mustard oil in their cooking. It was discovered that the oil had been made from poisonous prickly poppy seeds, which look and taste like mustard seeds.

CAN HONEY TURN ROTTEN?
Honey is antibacterial and never goes bad.

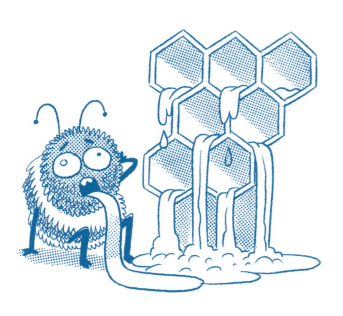

HOW DID GRAPEFRUITS GET THEIR NAME?
Grapefruits got their name from the way they grow in clusters that look like bunches of huge grapes!

Chew On This

DID YOU KNOW?
A study at Harvard University found that drinking hot chocolate can help your memory.

HOW MUCH TEA IS DRUNK IN BRITAIN?
Around 100 million cups every day! The average Brit drinks 23 times more tea than the average Italian.

CAN EATING CARROTS TURN YOU ORANGE?
Yes. Eating large amounts will turn your skin orange ... but you need to eat a lot of them!

DID YOU KNOW?
Until the 18th century, English people believed tomatoes were poisonous.

Chew On This

WHERE CAN YOU GET BLUE FRIES?
Salad Blue and Blue Congo are types of potatoes. They make blue fries!

WHAT SPIKY FEAST WAS ENJOYED IN THE MIDDLE AGES?
Hedgehogs were eaten in medieval times and are still a source of food in some countries. One way to cook them is in clay—when the baked clay is broken off, the spines come with it.

WHO OWNED A CHOCOLATE CAR?
A Chinese car dealer covered a Volkswagen Beetle in 200 kg (440 lb) of chocolate for his Valentine's Day display!

WHAT SMELL CAN HELP YOU CONCENTRATE?
The lovely smell of lemons can help you concentrate! A study using the citrus aroma in cars showed that drivers performed much better than they did without it.

Chew On This

WHO BANNED SAUSAGES?
The early Catholic church banned sausages, since they were traditionally eaten during pagan festivals.

DID YOU KNOW?
Carrot jam is a delicacy in Portugal.

WHO EATS THE MOST EGGS?
Egg consumption varies a lot between countries. In 2018, the average Mexican ate 368 eggs, while the average Indian ate only 76.

HOW OLD ARE NOODLES?
The remains of 4,000-year-old noodles were found at a site in China in 2005, settling the argument of where they were invented!

Chew On This

WHERE IS CELERY ILLEGAL?

Throwing celery onto the field was a tradition for fans of the English football team Chelsea. When it became a crime, one arrested fan vowed never to eat celery again!

IS CHEWING GUM GOOD FOR YOU?

Japanese scientists believe that chewing gum is good for your brain. Chewing stimulates the brain and can actually improve your memory!

IS THERE A KIND OF RICE THAT IS FORBIDDEN?

Forbidden rice is a black rice grain that becomes dark purple when cooked, and turns the water it is cooked in bright purple.

CAN VEGETARIANS EAT MARSHMALLOWS?

Marshmallow got its name from the plant of the same name. The first marshmallows contained the plant extract as its gelling agent, but modern forms use gelatin. This makes them unsuitable for vegetarians and vegans, since gelatin is made from boiled-up animal parts!

Chew On This

WHO WAS PAID WITH SALT?
Salt was highly prized by the Romans—soldiers were sometimes paid in salt, which is how the word "salary" originated.

DID YOU KNOW?
Fried cod tongues are a popular Norwegian delicacy.

WHO BAKED FASHION?
For one of his exhibitions, designer Jean Paul Gaultier had dresses, shoes, and hats specially made ... by bakers! His show was called Pain Couture, and the exhibits were made from bread and pastry.

HOW IS MAPLE SYRUP MADE?
It takes 40 l (85 pt) of sap from a maple tree to make 1 l (2.1 pt) of maple syrup.

Chew On This

WHO WAS SERVED A TATTOOED PIZZA?
A Welshman celebrated the opening of his new pizza restaurant by having a slice of ham and pineapple pizza tattooed on the back of his head! His tattoo took three hours, and the event raised money for charity.

DID YOU KNOW?
An English fisherman saved an edible crab ... because it had three claws! Instead of ending up as lunch, Claudette the mutant crustacean went on show at the local aquarium.

HOW MANY TYPES OF MUSTARD ARE THERE?
The National Mustard Museum in Wisconsin, USA, has a collection of over 6,000 different types of mustard!

CAN YOU GROW BRAZIL NUTS ON FARMS?
No. Brazil nuts only grow in rain forests.

Chew On This

CAN DOGS EAT NOODLES?
They can—but they probably shouldn't. After a Chinese man fed instant noodles to his dogs too often, they became addicted and refused to eat anything else!

CAN YOU WEAR BANANAS?
Banana plants have been used to make cloth for hundreds of years in Japan.

DID YOU KNOW?
Garbanzo beans—also called chickpeas—were used as a coffee substitute during the World War I.

WHAT DESSERT WAS TOPS WITH NERO?
Roman Emperor Nero liked his iced desserts! He would send slaves to the mountains to fetch snow, which would then be mixed with fruit, nuts, and honey.

Chew On This

WHERE CAN YOU FIND SNAKES IN WINE?

Vietnamese snake wine is a large bottle of rice wine ... with a cobra coiled up inside it! It is sold for its medicinal properties.

DID YOU KNOW?

It's good to eat varied foods, but people can survive on very strange diets. A British man lived mainly on cheese for 20 years.

HOW DO YOU MAKE RICE "PUFF?"

Puffed rice is made from grains of rice that have been heated until they bubble up to produce thin outer walls. The noise you hear when you pour milk on your cereal is those walls collapsing from the moisture!

ARE ALL CARROTS ORANGE?

Until the 17th century, carrots were purple. Now you can choose to eat orange, red, yellow, or white ones, too!

Chew On This

HOW MUCH SUGAR IS IN COLA?
A can of cola contains the equivalent of seven teaspoons of sugar.

DID YOU KNOW?
The first ketchup was made with pickled fish in East Asia.

HOW MUCH OF CAMBODIA IS RICE PADDIES?
About 90 percent of Cambodia's agricultural land is used to grow rice.

WHY DO PEOPLE CALL SOME VEGETABLES "EGGPLANTS?"
Eggplants (sometimes known as aubergines) got their strange name because some types are not purple but white, and as the fruits are growing, they look like eggs!

Chew On This

DID YOU KNOW?
Watermelon rinds are edible. They are used as a vegetable in Asian stir-fries and stews.

WHAT DO YOU EAT ON FAT THURSDAY?
In Poland and Germany, the last Thursday before Lent is known as Fat Thursday, and it's a day when people stuff themselves with cakes!

WHAT'S THE RECORD FOR EGG YOLKS?
The largest chicken egg recorded had five yolks in it!

DID YOU KNOW?
The tea in tea bags is the waste product left over from the sorting of higher-quality loose-leaf tea. The stuff in tea bags is known as dust.

WHERE DID COFFEE USED TO BE SOLD?
In many countries, coffee used to be sold in pharmacies. It was known as Arabian wine.

Chew On This

DID YOU KNOW?
The Australian finger lime has the widest variation of any citrus fruit—it can be green, red, orange, yellow, purple, black, or brown!

WHICH EGG TAKES THE LONGEST TO BOIL?
It takes around 40 minutes to hard-boil an ostrich egg!

WHAT MAKES THE STRAWBERRY SPECIAL?
The strawberry is the only fruit that has its seeds on its outer skin.

WHO ATE SWANS FOR CHRISTMAS?
A medieval Christmas dinner for the rich might consist of swan or peacock.

DID YOU KNOW?
Despite being a cancer-causing substance, talcum powder is still used in some countries to coat rice to improve its appearance. Talc-coated rice is banned in the USA.

Chew On This

WHAT ARE THE BUBBLES IN BUBBLE TEA?

Bubble tea, or pearl tea, is a popular Asian tea drink. What makes it unusual is that it has big, black, chewy tapioca balls swimming around in it that sink to the bottom of the cup!

IS GARLIC DANGEROUS?

Garlic that has been stored in oil for too long can produce the highly toxic botulism poison.

DID YOU KNOW?

Until the 20th century, lobster was seen as a food for the poor and was even used as fertilizer!

WHERE MIGHT YOU BE SERVED CHICKEN NECK SKIN?

Chicken neck skin is sometimes used as a casing for kosher sausages.

Chew On This

DID YOU KNOW?
People train pig-tailed macaque monkeys to collect coconuts in parts of Asia.

WHICH US PRESIDENT KEPT A COW?
Milk for US President William Taft and his family was provided by a cow that grazed freely on the White House lawn!

WHO ATE LETTUCE FOR DESSERT?
The Romans used to eat lettuce as a dessert.

WHO GAVE THEIR EMPTY PLATES TO THE POOR?
Trenchers were medieval plates made from stale bread. When the meal was finished, the trenchers would be given to the poor to eat. How generous!

DID YOU KNOW?
Medieval wafers were made with coats of arms imprinted on them.

Chew On This

WHERE CAN YOU HAVE BRAINS FOR BREAKFAST?

Brains 'n' eggs is a Southern United States' dish made with scrambled eggs and pig's brain. Yummy!

WHAT'S INSIDE ITALIAN CIBREO SAUCE?

Italian cibreo is a sauce made from cockscombs (rooster head crests) and chicken livers.

DID YOU KNOW?

French soups sold in the street were called *restaurers* for their restorative properties. The first restaurant opened in Paris in 1765, selling the soups and providing tables to eat them at.

DID YOU KNOW?

Frost is necessary in the growth of parsnips. It helps develop their taste.

WHAT IS A FUZZY MELON?

A fuzzy melon is an Asian vegetable similar to squash.

Awesome Animals

WHAT TINY CRITTER CAN LIVE IN A TENNIS BALL?

A used tennis ball can be turned into a home for the humble harvest mouse. With these mice's natural habitat disappearing due to intensive farming methods, the UK Wildlife Trust decided to provide new homes for them. The Trust took old tennis balls from Wimbledon (where a famous tennis tournament is held), cut out an entrance, and left a seed inside as bait, before suspending the balls above the ground, out of reach from predators.

DID YOU KNOW?
Hummingbirds are the only type of bird that can fly backward.

WHAT IS THE WORLD'S LUCKIEST FROG?

Nong Oui, a black-spotted female frog, became a celebrity in Pattaya, Thailand, when she learned how to sit on a toy motorcycle. But one of Nong's other talents has caused a bigger stir. Her owner claimed that the frog could predict the national lottery numbers, proving it by choosing the winning numbers for 10 lotteries in a row.

WHICH ANIMAL LIVED THE LONGEST?

Addwaitya the giant tortoise was thought to be the world's oldest animal when he died. He lived in India and reached the grand old age of 255. His 1.5 m (5 ft)-wide shell later went on display at a local museum.

Awesome Animals

CAN YOU TEACH A RAT TO SURF?

Apparently, yes! In Hawaii, two rats, Fin and Tofu, regularly headed out to tackle the waves. Their young owner, Boomer Hodel, took them surfing twice a week for 20 minutes at a time, cresting 1.2-m (4-ft) waves and performing tricks, such as surfing through "tubes" (tunnels of water). Boomer discovered that his rats loved water when he took them to the beach to wash them. He created two mini boards, so the reckless rodent duo could perfect their surfing skills.

WHICH RODENT IS A REAL TOUGH NUT?

Large rodents named agoutis are the only animals that can open Brazil nuts with their teeth.

DID YOU KNOW?

The harvest mouse (*Micromys minutus*) is Britain's tiniest mouse. It only weighs about the same as a small coin.

ARE RATS GOOD SWIMMERS?

Very! In 2005, an escaped radio-tagged rat took off from the coast of New Zealand. Scientists studying the rat recorded him swimming for 400 m (1,312 ft) before they recaptured him!

Awesome Animals

HOW DID THE GUINEA PIG GET ITS NAME?

It is believed that the English name for the rodent, "guinea," came from the amount of money you had to pay for the furball when it was first introduced to Britain. A guinea was a British coin used in the late 1600s and 1700s.

CAN ARMADILLOS SWIM?

An armadillo can stay underwater for up to six minutes! First, it needs to fill its stomach with air, otherwise it would sink under the weight of its heavy body plating.

HOW SPORTY ARE PIGS?

Pigs have their own Olympic Games! Entrants compete in events such as an obstacle race, pigball (where a ball is covered in fish oil to encourage the pigs to push it toward a goal), and piggy paddling or wading from one side of a pool to the other. Unfortunately, the competitors are usually better at colliding with each other than swimming in a straight line!

Awesome Animals

WHERE ARE GUINEA PIGS TREATED LIKE KINGS?

Guinea pigs are a popular pet in the Western world, but in the home of its ancestors, it is treated very differently. In Huacho, Peru, locals dress up the rodents in traditional Peruvian costumes for the annual Festival of the Guinea Pig. They can be dressed up as miners, peasants, folk singers, and kings, with a prize for the best costume.

ARE HAMSTERS INDESTRUCTIBLE?

Sadly not, but one cute critter managed to survive an ordeal most would scamper from. In 2006, a hamster named Mike survived a journey through a shredder and three different kinds of crushing machines during his death-defying journey at an industrial waste unit in Wales. He was spun, shaken, and nearly crushed to death before popping out of the other end of the four-minute process, normally used to take apart washing machines. Workers were amazed to find him in one piece, with just a sore foot to show for his ordeal.

DON'T THEY EAT GUINEA PIGS IN PERU?

Yes, but they don't dress them for dinner! In Peru, the small rodent is called *cuy*. It is a very popular dish, served up fried, roasted, baked, or grilled. There is even a contest in the Festival of the Guinea Pig for the tastiest dish!

DID YOU KNOW?

Slugs have two noses! One is located on the head and is used for smelling, and the other is on the tail and is used for breathing. Snails also use their eyes for smelling!

Awesome Animals

CAN SQUIRRELS WATER SKI?

Yes, though they do need to train. A number of squirrels, all named Twiggy, have been trained to water ski by Chuck and Lou Ann Best of Florida, USA, since the late 1970s. Their very first squirrel was found as a baby after a hurricane had blown it out of its nest. Then, after buying a remote-controlled boat, Chuck thought it might be a good idea to train the squirrel to ski behind it! Twiggy the squirrel took to the skis like a pro, and he and his successors have appeared on many TV shows, in commercials, and even starred in hit Hollywood movies such as *Dodgeball* and *Anchorman*.

IS IT JUST SQUIRRELS THAT CAN WATER SKI?

No. Chuck and Lou Ann Best also trained an armadillo, two French poodles, and two miniature horses to water ski. They taught a chimpanzee to roller-skate, too!

DID YOU KNOW?

You needed to carry a lot of balls to play fetch with Dallas, Texas, golden retriever Augie. She could hold five tennis balls in her mouth at once!

WHERE CAN YOU FIND THE WORLD'S UGLIEST DOG?

The World's Ugliest Dog Festival at the Sonoma-Marin fair in Petaluma, California, USA, is the place! Dog owners from across the country travel to the contest to show off their pets' "challenging" looks. The 2008 winner, Gus from Florida, had just one eye after a fight with a tomcat, no hair at all, and only three legs after his ongoing battle with skin cancer. The $1,600 prize money came in handy for paying for Gus's radiation treatment!

Awesome Animals

DID YOU KNOW?
Every dog has a unique nose print.

ARE DOGS CREATIVE?
Have you heard of a pooch Picasso? Britain's Shore Service Dogs have been raising money by selling their mutt masterpieces. Trained by their owner, Mary Stadelbacher, the dogs paint bright and "abstract" paintings by holding the brush in their mouths. The resulting work has fetched up to £230 (about $300) per picture.

HOW TINY IS THE WORLD'S SMALLEST DOG?
The smallest recorded living dog is a chihuahua from Orlando, Florida, USA. Teeny Pearl measures just 9.14 cm (3.6 in) tall. When she was born in September 2020, she weighed less than 28 g (1 oz), and could fit in a teaspoon! Pearl's aunt, named Miracle Milly, was the previous holder of the world record.

CAN DOGS GET MARRIED?
For fun, yes. In Littleton, Colorado, USA, a mass mutt wedding was arranged, with owners arriving along with 356 dogs. The dogs swapped their usual collars for full-blown wedding clothes, including tuxedos and wedding dresses. Perfect puppy pairings were arranged with the help of a pet marriage consultant. For pooch owners with cash to splash, a wedding planner charged £720 (about $925) to source smart outfits for the special day, while providing a marriage certificate and even a cake.

Awesome Animals

HOW LONG CAN A HORSE'S TAIL GROW?

The owner of Summer the American paint horse had to keep her beloved animal's tail braided and covered in a tube sock when she was not showing her off, otherwise it dragged on the ground! The tail in question measured a mighty 3.81 m (12.5 ft). Summer's extraordinary tail was combed and shampooed every two months. The owner, Crystal Socha, had to put aside three hours to accomplish this task because each hair was as fine as a fishing line!

DID YOU KNOW?

A sick Yorkshire terrier was found by a vet to have swallowed eight party balloons. After they were removed, it must have felt a little deflated!

IS THERE A FAT CAT CHAMPION?

Tiddles, a stray cat adopted by June Watson of the UK, claimed the title of London Fat Cat Champion. Weighing the same as a six-year-old boy, Tiddles became a star who received letters and the finest cuisine from many fans.

HOW HEAVY IS THE WORLD'S FATTEST CAT?

No official records are recorded now, to discourage owners from overfeeding their pets, but when records were kept, Katy, a Siamese cat living in the Ural mountains in Russia, was off the charts. Despite her owner claiming that she "didn't eat much," Katy weighed a cat-aclysmic 22.5 kg (50 lb).

Awesome Animals

HOW CAN FLESH-EATING FISH BE GOOD FOR YOU?

Garra rufa fish are tiny fish that love to peck the dry skin off your feet. Used medically in the treatment of ailments such as eczema, the fish are also used in salons to help give customers pedicures. Clients sit with their bare feet dipped into a tank while the tiny toothless carp help remove the dead skin from their toes over a 15-30-minute session.

ARE THERE HORSES AS SMALL AS DOGS?

Yes, and small dogs, at that! Tiny Thumbelina was the world's smallest horse ever at only 44 cm (17 in) across. This dwarf miniature horse was nicknamed Mini Mini by her owner, Michael Goessling. Not only was she dog-sized, but Thumbelina liked the company of hounds as well as the other 50 horses in Goessling's stable.

DID YOU KNOW?

Horses can't breathe through their mouths—they can only breathe through their noses.

WHICH MONKEY IS THE FASTEST ON LAND?

The African patas monkey can race along the ground at 55 km/h (34 mph), making it not just the fastest monkey on land, but also the fastest primate.

Awesome Animals

DID YOU KNOW?
Goats can learn their name and be trained to come when they are called.

CAN GOATS CLIMB TREES?
Yes. Just as goats can nimbly clamber up cliffs and over rocky mountains, there are goats in Morocco that climb the local Argan trees to gobble up delicious berries. And no, they don't use ladders.

HOW MANY WORDS CAN A BIRD LEARN TO REPEAT?
Puck the budgerigar knew a record 1,728 words before he died in 1994.

WHO RUBS GOAT POOP ON THEIR SKIN?
Once the same goats have eaten their fill up in the Argan trees, they poop out the kernels of the berry seed. These kernels are picked up by the locals and ground to make Argan oil. You can then buy the oil and use it in the kitchen or rub it on your skin as a beauty treatment! Of course, Argan oil can also be produced using modern machinery directly from the berries, but for some, the old ways are the best.

Awesome Animals

CAN CHIMPS DO KARATE?

Yes—27-year-old Charlie the chimpanzee was the proud recipient of a karate black belt. His owner, Carmen Presti, noticed the chimp's interest in martial arts when Carmen was working out at a local karate studio. Soon, Charlie began picking up the moves, including kicking and punching. After being awarded a black belt for his amazing skills, Charlie toured the USA. His jump-spinning heel kicks were a sensation on talk shows and commercials.

HOW ABOUT CHOPPING PLANKS IN HALF?

While Charlie could high kick, a 12-year-old monkey in Japan had the power to karate-chop panels of wood in two. When he wasn't sparring with his sensei (martial arts teacher), the monkey would serve drinks at his sensei's bar. Yachan was trained by his monkey-breeding owner on a daily basis, and did sit-ups, push-ups, and rope jumping.

CAN SPIDERS SPIN WEBS IN SPACE?

Yes. Spiders Arabella and Anita were the first to spin webs in space in 1973. The pair were transported to the US space station Skylab. Sadly, both spidernauts died while in Earth orbit. A year later, their bodies were returned to Earth and donated to the Smithsonian's National Air and Space Museum for display.

WHICH SPIDER WEAVES THE TOUGHEST WEB?

The American *Achaearanea tepidariorum* spider has the strongest known web. It is tough enough to ensnare a mouse.

Awesome Animals

WHICH COUNTRY IS PLAGUED WITH GIANT TOADS?

Australia has a plague of poisonous cane toads, which can grow to be the size of a small dog. The Aussie government has asked people to kill them humanely, but most Australians just bash them over the head!

DO SPIDERS MAKE NOISE?

Some do. The noisiest spider is the European buzzing spider. The male makes a buzzing sound as it vibrates its abdomen against a leaf to attract a mate.

DID YOU KNOW?

Squirrels can climb trees faster than they can run on the ground!

WHAT IS THE WORLD'S TOUGHEST CREATURE?

The most heat-tolerant organism lives under superhigh pressure and in boiling hot hydrothermal vents at the bottom of the Pacific Ocean. Bacteria-like Strain 121 can survive temperatures of 121 °C (250 °F).

55

Awesome Animals

WHICH ANIMAL HAS THE LONGEST MIGRATION IN THE WORLD?

The tiny Arctic tern has the longest migration of any animal. It breeds in the Arctic, flies south to Antarctica during the northern winter, then flies back again!

CAN YOU RACE ON A BUFFALO?

At the annual water buffalo festival in Chonburi, Thailand, jockeys race on buffalo along a "drag" strip roughly 100 m (330 ft) long. Riders race along the course with no saddle or stirrups, clinging on to the buffalo's loose skin for dear life as the animals either rush down to the finish line or decide to do their own thing and not bother finishing. Or worse still, they think that the best way of dealing with such a race is to do everything possible to throw the jockey off their backs!

DID YOU KNOW?
The gecko is the only lizard that makes noises.

ARE DONKEYS SPEEDY?

Donkeys are not known for their speed, but donkey racing is very popular the world over. From kids racing them at Dunton Stables in West Midlands, UK, and the donkey derbies featured in festivals all over the world (including Santas racing donkeys in the Swiss Alps), through to professional jockeys competing in Hanover, Germany, donkey racing is a big deal. One winning racing donkey was sold for £25,000 (about $32,075).

Awesome Animals

IS IT POSSIBLE TO RIDE AN OSTRICH?

You can not only ride, but race on the biggest of birds! Those brave enough to attempt ostrich racing do look utterly ridiculous in the process, though. For some, such as the ostrich farmer workers based at the Highgate Ostrich Farm in Oudtshoorn, South Africa, racing is a daily event, as they take to the track to show spectators just how quickly the ostriches can move. A rider-less ostrich can run as fast a racehorse, with a top speed of 64 km/h (40 mph).

DID YOU KNOW?

Ostriches are the largest and heaviest birds in the world, as well as being the fastest.

DO FLEAS REALLY PERFORM IN CIRCUSES?

These tiny insects can really perform amazing feats. The annual Floh-Circus in Munich, Germany, is home to a show where fleas are put through their paces across a wide range of disciplines. These include flea soccer, where the insect "kicks" a tiny ball into a net, and a flea-powered chariot race. The dog fleas used are able to pull objects that are an astonishing 20,000 times heavier than themselves.

WHICH ANIMAL TRAVELS 3,100 MILES IN A YEAR?

North American caribou deer travel up to 5,000 km (3,106 mi) a year on their annual route in search of food.

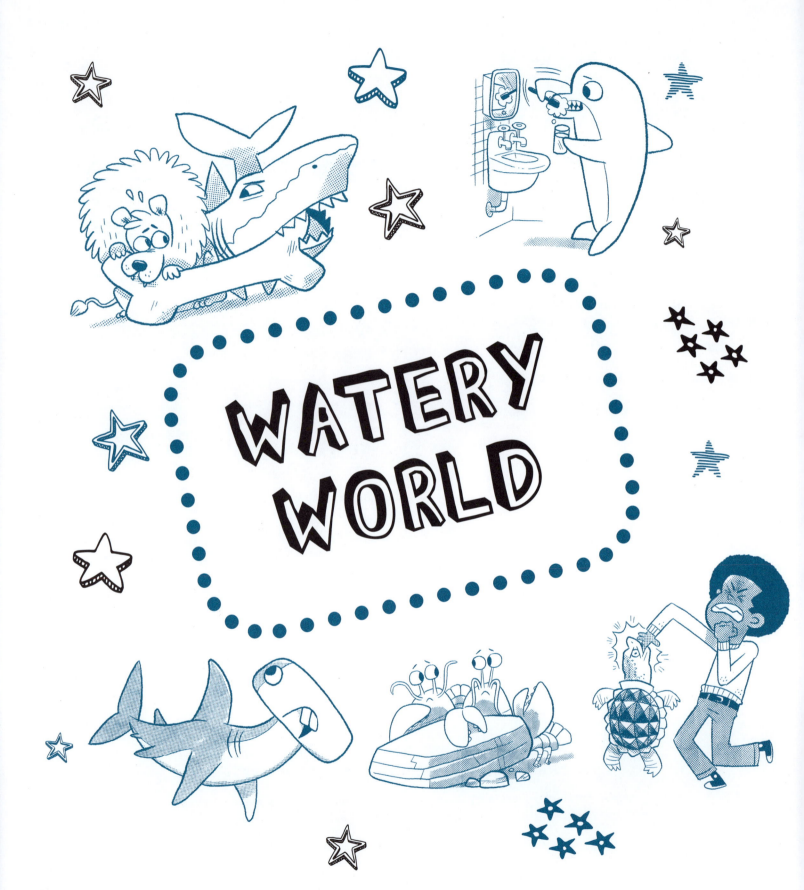

Watery World

WHICH CREATURE HAS THE MOST POWERFUL PUNCH?

The peacock mantis shrimp has the strongest animal punch! Its front leg moves at 23 m (75 ft) per second to club its prey.

HOW HEAVY IS A BLUE WHALE?

A blue whale can weigh up to 125 metric tons (138 tons). That's as much as 23 elephants, 230 cows, or 1,800 adult men.

WHAT IS THE LARGEST ANIMAL IN THE WORLD ... EVER?

The blue whale is the largest creature known to have lived on our planet—bigger than any dinosaur. The longest blue whale ever found measured just over 33 m (110 ft). That's the length of nine family cars end to end!

DID YOU KNOW?

The arteries of the massive blue whale are so huge that a human baby could crawl through them.

Watery World

ARE DOLPHINS WHALES?
Yes. The two main types of whales are whales with teeth and whales without teeth. Dolphins are toothed whales. Other toothed whales include sperm whales and belugas. Orcas, also known as killer whales, are a type of dolphin.

HOW MANY TYPES OF DOLPHINS ARE THERE?
Experts cannot agree on an exact figure, but there are about 40. One problem is that not everyone agrees on which species are dolphins. Another is that some kinds are rare and are dying out.

HOW DO YOU MAKE A SHARK EXPLODE?
Killer whales have been known to attack sharks by launching themselves into their prey's stomach, like a torpedo. The force of the impact can cause the shark to explode.

DID YOU KNOW?
Sharks will eat anything, even parts of their own bodies that have been bitten after an attack by another animal.

Watery World

DID YOU KNOW?
If a dolphin loses its tail, scientists can attach an artificial rubber tail made from the same material used to make Formula 1 car tires. It's proven to work as well as the real thing!

HOW MANY TEETH DO DOLPHINS HAVE?

Dolphins have wide, cone-shaped teeth, just right for grasping slippery prey. One set of between 60 and 100 teeth lasts them a lifetime. The teeth start coming through when baby dolphins are about five weeks old.

WHICH ANIMALS EAT DOLPHINS?

Sharks eat dolphins. Many dolphins have shark-bite scars on their bodies, so at least some of them get away. Orcas eat dolphins, too—even though they belong to the same family.

WHAT ARE PORPOISES?

Porpoises are the smallest members of the whale family. They are only 1.5-2.5 m (5-8 ft) long. The harbor (or harbour) porpoise is the best known. It is found in cool, coastal waters all over the northern hemisphere.

Watery World

ARE ALL SHARK TEETH THE SAME?
Shark teeth come in different shapes to suit their owners' diets. Spear-like teeth are good for catching slippery fish and squid, while blunt teeth can crush shells. Great whites have triangular cutting teeth for slicing into seals.

DO SHARKS LIVE IN RIVERS?
Bull sharks swim far up rivers and into lakes, so they are more likely to meet (and eat) bathers and swimmers than sharks that stay out at sea. Bull sharks are widespread and found in the Amazon, Zambezi, and Ganges rivers.

DID YOU KNOW?
Great white sharks have a bite three times more powerful than that of an African lion.

HOW BIG DO GREAT WHITE SHARKS GET?
Great white sharks can grow up to 6.1 m (20 ft) long. Females are, on average, about 1 m (3 ft) longer than males.

Watery World

WHY DO HAMMERHEAD SHARKS LOOK SO ODD?

Hammerhead sharks have wide, hammer-shaped heads with eyes on the tips. Swinging their heads from side to side gives them amazing all-around vision. During the day, hammerheads often rest together in large groups of up to 100.

WHAT EATS SHARKS?

Sharks are apex predators, which means that they have no natural predators of their own. However, sharks are still at risk from being eaten—by other, bigger sharks!

WHAT IS A SAW SHARK?

Saw sharks are extremely rare. They have wide, flat bodies, but their distinguishing feature is a long, narrow snout studded with pointed teeth. The sharks use this "saw" to slash at fish or to probe the seabed for shellfish.

DO CARPET SHARKS LIVE ON FLOORS?

Some sharks have mottled markings that look like carpet patterns and help camouflage them. The tasselled wobbegong is one of the strangest carpet sharks. Its seaweed-like tentacles swish in the current, disguising the shark and attracting prey.

Watery World

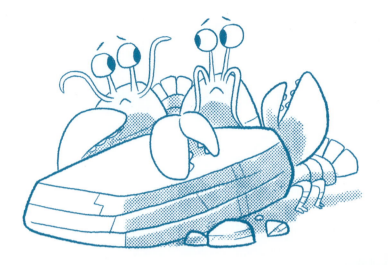

WHAT ARE LOBSTERS AFRAID OF?

Lobsters are scared of octopuses. Even the sight of one is enough to make a lobster freeze in horror.

DID YOU KNOW?

An octopus will sometimes eat its own arms and even its own body, if it becomes extremely stressed.

WHAT HAPPENS WHEN AN OCTOPUS LOSES AN ARM?

If an octopus loses an arm, it can grow a new one! Even after it has been cut off, an octopus arm will continue wriggling for some time.

DOES AN OCTOPUS HAVE MORE THAN ONE HEART?

Octopuses have three hearts! Two pump blood through its gills to help it breathe, while the third pumps blood around the rest of its body.

Watery World

DID YOU KNOW?

Octopuses have been known to remove the stinging tentacles from jellyfish and use them as weapons.

CAN OCTOPUSES CHANGE SHAPE?

The mimic octopus can change its shape and hue in order to scare off predators. It has been known to make itself look like a very convincing sea snake.

WHICH SEA CREATURE HAS THE LARGEST EYES?

The vampire squid has the largest eyes of any animal in relation to its body size. If it was the size of a human, it would have eyes the size of table tennis paddles!

WHY DID DENTISTS LIKE STINGRAYS?

Ancient Greek dentists used the venom from stingrays' spines as an anesthetic.

Watery World

HOW BIG CAN SQUID GROW?

The largest giant squid ever caught was a whopping 13 m (43 ft) long and weighed almost 1 metric ton (1.1 tons). Its body was so enormous that calamari rings (squid rings) made from it would have been the size of truck tires!

DID YOU KNOW?

The jaws of a snapping turtle are so powerful that they can rip off a human finger.

DID YOU KNOW?

Instead of black ink, some species of deep-sea squid squirt a cloud of glowing, luminous ink to distract predators in the dark depths of the ocean.

IS THERE REALLY A COOKIECUTTER SHARK?

Yes. The cookiecutter shark is named for its unusual feeding method. It bites circular chunks out of larger animals, such as dolphins and whales. The wounds eventually heal, leaving the victims with 5 cm (2 in)-diameter round scars.

Watery World

WHAT IS THE LARGEST CRAB IN THE WORLD?

The largest of all crustaceans is the Japanese spider crab. Its body is about 37 cm (15 in) across, but its legs are like stilts, spanning up to 3.81 m (12.5 ft).

WHERE CAN YOU FIND MONSTER CRABS?

The Barents Sea is teeming with monster Kamchatka crabs after they were introduced in the 1960s to provide a fishing source for Russian fishermen. The gigantic crustaceans can measure more than 1 m (3 ft) from claw to claw.

DID YOU KNOW?

The North Atlantic lobster grows up to 60 cm (24 in) long and can weigh up to 20 kg (44 lb), making it the heaviest crustacean that lives in the sea.

ARE PREHISTORIC CRABS STILL ALIVE TODAY?

Horseshoe crabs are "living fossils." They first appeared on Earth in the Carboniferous period, 300-355 million years ago. Little has changed about their appearance since then, as fossils from the late Jurassic era show.

Watery World

HOW DO YOU ESCAPE A MORAY EEL?
If you're bitten by a moray eel, the only way to get away is to kill it by cutting off its head and breaking its jaws. It won't let go while it's alive.

WHAT IS A JELLYFISH MADE OF?
A jellyfish is 95 percent water—the same as a cucumber! It is not as tasty in a salad, though!

DID YOU KNOW?
The lamprey, an eel-like creature, has no jaws. To eat, it attaches its sucker mouth to another fish, then literally sucks all the fluids out of it, killing the fish by sucking it dry.

HOW SHOCKING IS AN ELECTRIC EEL?
Electric eels can deliver a shock of 500 volts to stun their prey into submission. The electricity supplied to your home is only 240 volts! You could power two refrigerators with the electricity produced by a single electric eel.

Watery World

HOW DOES A SEA STAR EAT?
A sea star can turn its stomach inside out by pushing it through its mouth.

WHICH FISH IS LIKE A VACUUM CLEANER?
Some grouper fish are so huge that when they open their mouths they create a suction that pulls prey straight into their gaping maws.

HOW BRAINY IS A SEA STAR?
A sea star doesn't have a brain. An extremely complex nerve system called the nerve plexus controls its arms instead.

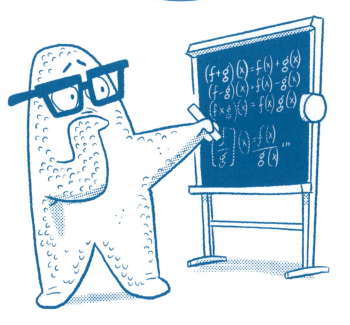

IS THERE A SEA UNICORN?
The long horn of the narwhal is actually an extended tooth! The animal's other name, "unicorn of the sea," isn't really correct, because it has no horn!

Watery World

WHICH FISH CARRIES ITS OWN LAMP IN FRONT OF ITS FACE?

The anglerfish lives in the darkest depths of the sea and has a glowing blob, like a little lantern, dangling in front of its head! The deep-sea anglerfish's lure glows in the dark, so it can be seen through the gloom and tempt prey to come near.

DID YOU KNOW?

Some deepwater fish can live for up to 150 years! And scientists have found a deepwater coral that is more than 4,000 years old.

WHICH FISH HAS SEE-THROUGH TEETH?

The viperfish has transparent, extra-long, razorlike teeth that cannot be seen in the dark, but it has to open its jaws almost vertically to catch prey. The teeth of a viperfish are half the length of its head, so it can't close its mouth, either! It has to open its jaws very wide in order to swallow.

DID YOU KNOW?

Some creatures thrive in the most inhospitable places. In the darkness of the deep ocean, colonies of Pompeii worms live on boiling-hot volcanic vents, like steaming chimneys on the seabed. Named after the site of a disastrous volcanic eruption in ancient Rome, the worms build crusty tubes to live in and poke their heads out to feed on bacteria.

Watery World

DO MALE OR FEMALE SEAHORSES GET PREGNANT?

Male seahorses! The babies grow for three weeks in a pouch before the male gives birth to up to 200 of them over 72 hours. The effort leaves him looking drained—unsurprisingly!

DID YOU KNOW?

Stargazer fish are like super electric eels. As well as delivering electric shocks, they also have two poisonous spines on their backs. Scary!

WHAT'S THE OLDEST ANIMAL EVER FOUND?

A quahog clam found off the coast of Iceland in 2007 has been identified as being between 405 and 410 years old, making it the oldest animal ever discovered. It was a baby when Elizabeth I was on the throne in England (1558-1603) and was almost 350 years old by the end of the World War II!

WHAT IS THE WORLD'S LONGEST BONY FISH?

The four species of oarfish are true monsters of the deep. The giant oarfish is the world's longest bony fish. It usually grows to about 9 m (30 ft), but there have been reports of fish as long as 17 m (55 ft). That's as long as three school buses parked end to end!

Watery World

WHY SHOULDN'T YOU EAT A BLUE TANG?
Despite its beautiful looks, the flesh of the blue tang fish is actually poisonous if eaten by humans or other fish.

HOW BIG CAN CLAMS GROW?
The *Tridacna* clam has been known to grow up to 1.2 m (4 ft) long and weigh up to 227 kg (500 lb). Not bad for a clam!

DID YOU KNOW?
The sailfish has a dorsal fin along most of its back that can be raised like a sail when it's excited.

WHICH SEA CREATURE HAS A HUNDRED EYES?
A scallop has about 100 eyes around the edge of its shell. They're very handy for spotting approaching predators!

Watery World

DO ALL FISH HAVE RED BLOOD?
Some fish in Antarctica have a natural antifreeze in their bodies that makes their blood appear white instead of red.

CAN FISH CHEW?
Because of the design of their jaws, fish can't actually chew—they swallow most of their food whole.

DID YOU KNOW?
A sea slug can eat a hydroid (an underwater stinging nettle) without being stung. The stinging chemical is absorbed into its skin and then stings anything that tries to eat the slug. Clever!

WHAT HAPPENS WHEN YOU PLAY CHESS WITH A SOLE?
If you place a sole (a type of flat fish) on a chessboard, it will take just four minutes to change its skin patterns to match the squares on the board.

Past Peculair

WHICH FRENCH KING IS BURIED IN SEVERAL PLACES?

The remains of Louis IX of France are in more than one place. Some of his entrails were buried where he died in Tunis, others are in Palermo, and one of his fingers is in Paris. The rest of his body disappeared in the 16th century.

DID YOU KNOW?

The murder rate in medieval England was around 10 times higher than it is today.

HOW DID RICHARD THE LIONHEART DIE?

Richard I of England (also known as Richard the Lionheart) died from an arrow wound that became gangrenous.

WHAT DID PEOPLE USE FOR CASH BEFORE COINS WERE MADE?

Before coins were invented, shells were used as money in many countries.

Past Peculair

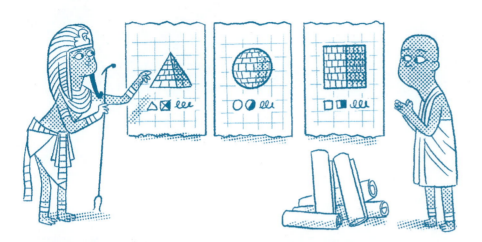

HOW DID ARGENTINA GET ITS NAME?

Argentina was named in the 16th century. The country is rich in silver, so the name came from the Latin for silver, *argentum*.

WHY IS A PYRAMID THAT SHAPE?

The shape of a pyramid represents the rays of the sun falling to Earth. The step formation was designed so that the dead Pharaoh inside could walk up to heaven on the sunrays!

DID YOU KNOW?

Until the 18th century, it was considered unmanly to eat with a fork.

WHO INVENTED THE SLINKY?

The Slinky toy was invented in the early 1940s after US engineer Richard James dropped a torsion spring and thought its movements were fun!

Past Peculair

WHO WAS NELSON MANDELA NAMED AFTER?

Nelson Mandela was the oldest elected president of South Africa, taking office at the age of 75. His first name was Rolihlahla, but a schoolteacher chose to call him Nelson instead, after Horatio Nelson.

WHEN WAS TOILET PAPER INVENTED?

The first factory-produced toilet paper became available in 1857 in the USA. People used all kinds of things before that—anything from leaves and fruit skins for the poor, to lace or wool for the rich!

DID YOU KNOW?

Play-Doh was originally sold in the 1930s as a product for cleaning soot off wallpaper.

WHEN WAS GLUE FIRST USED?

One of the first glues was made by the ancient Egyptians ... from boiled-up animal skins!

Past Peculair

DID YOU KNOW?
Gustave Eiffel originally intended to build his famous tower in Barcelona for the 1888 Universal Exposition, but his idea was rejected by city officials.

WHO WAS BURIED WITH 8,000 SOLDIERS?
The 5 km (3 mi)-long tomb of Chinese emperor Qin Shi Huang contains more than 8,000 life-size clay soldiers, created 2,300 years ago to protect him in the afterlife.

WHO HAD TO GIVE UP ALL THEIR TOYS AT 12?
In ancient times, children were considered to be grown-ups around the age of 12. They were expected to give up any toys when they reached "adulthood."

IS THE LEAD IN PENCILS ACTUALLY LEAD?
The lead in pencils has never contained lead! Pencils were developed from graphite sticks, which were used in the 16th century to mark sheep, and the first ones had casings made from string or sheepskin.

Past Peculair

WHERE WAS CHAMPAGNE INVENTED?
Champagne was invented in England, not France.

DID YOU KNOW?
The tug-of-war was an Olympic Games event between 1900 and 1920.

WHY WERE MANY ANCIENT EGYPTIANS BALD?
Some Ancient Egyptians shaved their heads to keep cool in the heat and to keep from getting lice.

WHICH AMERICAN PRESIDENT GOT STUCK IN THE BATHTUB?
US President William Howard Taft was a big man. So big, in fact, that he kept getting stuck in the White House bathtub, so a larger one had to be installed.

Past Peculair

IN WHICH COUNTRY WERE WOMEN FIRST GIVEN THE VOTE?

New Zealand became the first country to allow all its women to vote, in 1893.

DID YOU KNOW?

The *Titanic* sank in 1912, but its wreck was not located until 1985.

WHAT WAS GREEK FIRE USED FOR?

Greek fire was a weapon used by the Byzantine Greeks in naval battles. A stream of burning fluid that couldn't be put out with water was fired at enemy ships.

DID YOU KNOW?

The first man on the Moon, Neil Armstrong, was often travel sick as a child.

Past Peculair

WHO WAS NOT THE FIRST EUROPEAN TO REACH THE AMERICAS?

Christopher Columbus wasn't the first European explorer to reach the Americas. He had to abandon his 1492 voyage when his ship ran aground. He didn't get there until 1498—by which time others had beaten him to it!

WHERE DID CHRISTOPHER COLUMBUS END UP?

The remains of Christopher Columbus started off in Valladolid, Spain, and were moved several times to Seville, Santo Domingo, Havana, and back to Seville again!

DID YOU KNOW?

New Zealand mountaineer and one of the first people to climb Mount Everest, Sir Edmund Hillary spent his early adulthood as a beekeeper.

DID YOU KNOW?

Furnaces beneath the floors of buildings provided central heating systems in ancient times.

Past Peculair

WHO TOOK HIS PET POODLE INTO BATTLE WITH HIM?

Seventeenth-century aristocrat Prince Rupert of the Rhine took his large poodle dog into battle with him on several occasions.

WHO BECAME AN EMPEROR AS A CHILD?

Leo II became the Byzantine Emperor in 474 CE, when he was just seven years old!

WHERE WERE PRISONERS LOCKED IN A TREE?

The Boab Prison Tree is a huge hollow tree that was used to lock up prisoners on their way to Derby, Australia, during the 19th century.

DID YOU KNOW?

Jimmy Carter was the first US president to be born in a hospital.

Past Peculair

WHERE CAN YOU GO AND SEE A CENTURY-DEAD LEADER?

The waxy-looking embalmed body of Soviet leader Vladimir Lenin has been on display in Red Square, Moscow, in Russia, since he died in 1924.

DID YOU KNOW?

The bullet that killed Admiral Horatio Nelson in the Battle of Trafalgar in 1805 is on display in Windsor Castle, in England.

HOW DID VIKINGS CELEBRATE SUCCESS IN BATTLE?

Vikings used to drink from the skulls of their defeated enemies.

WHAT WERE EARLY FALSE TEETH MADE OF?

Early false teeth were made from hippopotamus bone and dead people's teeth!

Past Peculair

DID YOU KNOW?
Writer Ernest Hemingway had a cat with six toes.

WHY DID CHAMPAGNE MAKERS WEAR MASKS?
Seventeenth-century bottles of champagne exploded so frequently that cellar workers wore iron masks for protection.

WHAT DO POPES WEAR AT THEIR CORONATION?
Popes normally wear a tiara made from gold or silver for their coronation, but in 1800 Pope Pius VII had to wear one made from papier-mâché, because of the turbulent political sitaution in Europe at that time!

WHAT MADE BIG BEN MISS NEW YEAR'S EVE?
Heavy snow slowed down the normally accurate Big Ben clock in London on New Year's Eve 1962, making it announce the New Year 10 minutes late.

Past Peculair

DID YOU KNOW?
Can openers were invented 50 years after tin cans.

DID YOU KNOW?
Before high-speed drills were invented, dentists used slow hand-operated drills on their patient's teeth. Ouch!

WHO INVENTED FIREWORKS?
The Chinese invented fireworks more than 2,000 years ago. The sound was believed to scare off evil spirits.

HOW DID THE NOBEL PRIZE START WITH A BANG?
The Nobel Peace Prize is named after Swedish chemist Alfred Nobel—the man who invented dynamite. Many historians believe that he established the prize in order to make amends for the use of his invention in war.

Past Peculair

WHO OFFERED HIS WHISKERS TO THE GODS?
The hair from a young Roman's first shave would be offered to the gods. Emperor Nero put his in a lovely pearl-studded gold box!

HOW LONG WAS THE FIRST HELICOPTER FLIGHT?
The first helicopter flight lasted 20 seconds, with the rotary wing aircraft managing to get 30 cm (1 ft) off the ground!

DID YOU KNOW?
French artist Henri de Toulouse-Lautrec broke both his legs in his early teens, and they stopped growing. Therefore, as an adult, he had a full-grown torso and child-size legs.

WHO INVENTED JEANS?
Levi Strauss invented jeans in the 1850s when he saw a need for hard-wearing trousers among miners. His first versions were made with sailcloth, then he imported a French material called serge de Nîmes ... which became shortened to denim.

Past Peculair

WHICH RUSSIAN CITY KEEPS CHANGING ITS NAME?

Within the space of 77 years, the Russian city of St. Petersburg had its name changed to Petrograd, then Leningrad, then back to St. Petersburg again.

DID YOU KNOW?
The name Wendy was invented by J. M. Barrie and first appeared in his children's book, Peter Pan.

WHY DID CHINESE COINS HAVE HOLES IN THE MIDDLE?

Ancient Chinese coins were rectangular with a hole in the middle. The hole was for stringing them together.

WHEN WAS THE FIRST NEWSPAPER PRINTED?

The first-ever newspaper was printed in 1605 and looked like a book.

Past Peculair

WHO WORE POOP IN THEIR HAIR?
Some ancient tribes used animal dung to stiffen their hair. And you thought gel was stinky!

WHO PROPOSED TO HIS FIANCÉE WITH DOTS AND DASHES?
Prolific American inventor Thomas Edison proposed to his wife in Morse code!

DID YOU KNOW?
Deer antlers were used in the Stone Age to make harpoons, axes, combs, and needles.

WHY DID VIKINGS CUT UP THEIR COINS?
Viking coins were valued for their weight. If a Viking had to pay less for something, they would clip a bit off their coin!

88

Past Peculair

WHEN WERE SUNGLASSES FIRST WORN?

Sunglasses were worn in China as long ago as the 12th century—they used pieces of smoky quartz as dark lenses. They were worn by judges in court to conceal facial expressions during interrogation rather than for protection against the sun!

WHEN WAS THE FIRST LIGHTHOUSE BUILT?

The first lighthouse was built in 285 BCE near Alexandria, Egypt. The light was created by a fire that had to be kept burning all night!

DID YOU KNOW?

India has not invaded another country in the last 10,000 years.

DID YOU KNOW?

Early concrete was made with volcanic ash.

Past Peculair

DID YOU KNOW?
Alexander the Great ordered his soldiers to shave off their beards in case the enemy used them as a handle to grab hold of!

HOW SHORT WAS THE SHORTEST WAR IN HISTORY?
The Anglo-Zanzibar War took place in 1896 and lasted between 38 and 45 minutes. The UK ultimately defeated the Zanzibar Sultinate.

DID YOU KNOW?
American astronaut Buzz Aldrin's mother's maiden name was Moon.

WHAT IS THE WORLD'S OLDEST SOCCER COMPETITION?
The FA Cup is the oldest soccer competition. The first final was in 1872 between teams called the Wanderers and the Royal Engineers. The Wanderers won 1-0!

Past Peculair

WHICH ENGLISH KING HAD TO MARRY HIS BROTHER'S WIFE?
King Henry VIII's first wife was chosen for him when he was 11 years old, following his brother's death. He was to marry his brother's widow when he was old enough.

DID YOU KNOW?
Even ancient Greek babies had rattles—hollow clay shapes had pieces of clay inside to make the rattle sound.

WHO FLEW ACROSS THE SEA ABOARD A DUCK?
French aviator Henri Fabre made the first seaplane in 1910. The strange invention flew tail-first and was named Le Canard—The Duck!

DID YOU KNOW?
Louis XIV became King of France at the age of four and went on to reign for 72 years.

Shocking Science

DID YOU KNOW?
Water is the only substance that occurs naturally in liquid, solid, and gas forms (water, ice, and steam).

WHAT HAPPENS WHEN LIGHTNING HITS A BEACH?
A bolt of lightning is so hot that if it hits sand, it can turn it into glass!

ARE ALL DESERTS SANDY?
No. About 80 percent of the world's deserts are rocky. Some are salt-covered, and a few are even icy.

HOW FAR DOES DUST TRAVEL?
Dust from Africa and China can end up in North America when it gets carried across the sea by the wind.

Shocking Science

DID YOU KNOW?
Liquid oxygen is sky blue.

WHERE DOES ALL THE WATER GO?
A trillion tons of the world's water evaporates each day in the sun. Luckily, it all comes down again when it rains!

CAN HUMANS MAKE ELECTRICITY?
Yes. Your nervous system is constantly sending signals around the body by using electrical impulses. These are transmitted by nerve cells called neurons.

DID YOU KNOW?
Scientists have created rice that contains human genes! Genetically modified rice was developed with a human liver gene and, more recently, saliva and breast milk proteins.

Shocking Science

WHO FIRST USED THE ALARM CLOCK?
The first alarm clocks were created for monks in the 14th century to make sure they didn't miss their morning prayers!

HOW CAN YOU SCRATCH A DIAMOND?
Diamonds are so hard that only other diamonds can scratch them.

DOES IT EVER GET ICY IN AUSTRALIA?
A freak summer hailstorm once left Australian capital Canberra under a blanket of ice. In some parts of the city, the ice was up to 1 m (3 ft) deep!

DID YOU KNOW?
The Earth is not completely spherical! It bulges in the middle—if you take a ball and squash it slightly from top to bottom, that is the shape of our planet.

Shocking Science

CAN YOU LOSE WEIGHT ON MARS?
Yes, and you don't even have to go on a diet! The gravity on Mars is less than 40 percent of that on Earth. On Mars, you would weigh much less than you do now!

DID YOU KNOW?
Less than 1 percent of all the water on our planet is drinkable.

IS SILVER GOOD FOR YOU?
Silver has antimicrobial properties and was used in many treatments before the invention of antibiotics. People would often put a silver coin in their milk to keep it from going sour!

WHAT IS CHALK MADE OF?
Chalk is made from the fossilized skeletons of tiny sea animals!

Shocking Science

IS THE ATLANTIC OCEAN GROWING?

Yes. The Atlantic Ocean is increasing in width by 3.81 cm (1.5 in) every year.

WHERE DO MOST OF THE WORLD'S PLANTS AND ANIMALS LIVE?

Rain forests cover only 2 percent of the world's surface, but more than 50 percent of all our plants and animals are found there. The rain forests are so dense with trees that it takes 10 minutes for rain to drip over leaves to reach the forest floor.

DID YOU KNOW?
Uranus was originally called the Georgian Planet, after English King George III.

WHY DID MARS GET ITS NAME?
The planet Mars was named after the Roman god of war, because it looks red—like blood!

Shocking Science

HOW MANY METEOR CRATERS ARE ON EARTH?

There are more than 150 giant craters around the world, left by fallen meteorites. The largest one is in Arizona, USA—it measures more than 1,250 m (4,100 ft) in diameter and was created around 50,000 years ago.

IS THERE SUCH A THING AS MOONLIGHT?

No. The light of the Moon is the reflection of sunlight off the Moon's surface.

DOES THE MOON HAVE QUAKES?

There are earthquakes on the Moon ... called moonquakes, of course! There are also icequakes in Antarctica.

DID YOU KNOW?

Mussels, as well as oysters, can produce pearls.

Shocking Science

WHERE CAN YOU STILL FIND THE SMALLPOX VIRUS?

There have been no cases of the deadly smallpox virus since 1978, but cultures of the virus are held at the Centers for Disease Control and Prevention in the United States and at the Institute of Virus Preparations in Siberia, Russia.

WHO STUDIED SCIENCE BEFORE SCIENTISTS?

Before the birth of the word "scientist" in 1833, scientists were known as "natural philosophers" or "men of science." (Women didn't get much of a chance to participate back then!)

DID YOU KNOW?

A hurricane the size of Earth has been raging over the planet Jupiter for the past 300 years or so!

HOW CAN YOU TELL IF IS AN EGG IS HARD-BOILED?

You can tell if an egg is hard-boiled by spinning it. If the egg is raw, the liquid contents will keep the egg from spinning within three rotations. If the inside is solid, it will continue spinning.

Shocking Science

HOW MUCH ENERGY DOES A SUPERNOVA PRODUCE?
An exploding star is known as a supernova, and it produces as much energy in a few months as the Sun would in its 10-billion-year lifetime.

HOW OLD IS THE SUN?
The Sun is 4.5 billion years old.

DID YOU KNOW?
The largest part—about 90 percent—of an iceberg is hidden beneath the sea's surface.

WHAT IS OBSIDIAN?
Volcanoes produce a kind of natural glass called obsidian. It can be formed into a fine cutting edge that is sharper than a steel scalpel blade that is used in cardiac surgery.

Shocking Science

WHO INVENTED THE FIRST VENDING MACHINE?
First-century engineer Hero of Alexandria invented the first vending machine. It dispensed holy water!

DID YOU KNOW?
Even if it is not taken out of its packaging, a disposable battery will lose up to 25 percent of its power in a year.

WHY SHOULD YOU NEVER LOOK DIRECTLY AT THE SUN?
Looking directly at the Sun can cause permanent damage to the eye's retina.

WHY ARE INCANDESCENT LIGHT BULBS SO WASTEFUL?
Incandescent light bulbs (the old-fashioned kind, where a wire is heated inside the bulb to create light) are extremely inefficient—90 percent of the power they use creates heat, so only 10 percent is used for the light itself.

Shocking Science

DID YOU KNOW?
Every rainbow is unique. Each rainbow is formed from light hitting your eye at a very precise angle. Someone standing next to you will see light coming from a slightly different angle than you and therefore see a different rainbow.

WHAT ARE METEORITES MADE OF?
The three main types of meteorite are made of stone, iron, or a mixture of the two.

HOW MANY EARTHQUAKES OCCUR IN A YEAR?
There are about 500,000 detectable earthquakes around the world each year.

WHAT IS SALT MADE FROM?
Believe it or not, it's made from two poisons—sodium and chlorine! However, when they combine as sodium chloride, they become a perfectly safe food.

Shocking Science

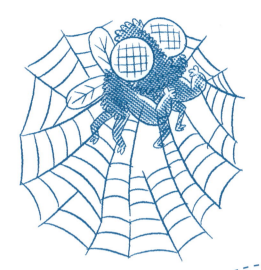

HOW STRONG IS SPIDER SILK?

It may look fragile, but spider silk is very strong—tougher than steel wire of the same thickness!

CAN YOU GET SUNBURNED ON THE MOON?

Yes. If you walked on the Moon without a space suit, you would get badly sunburned within a few seconds. Luckily, our planet's atmosphere keeps us from burning so quickly.

DID YOU KNOW?

Salt and vinegar is an explosive combination! There is a spectacular chemical reaction when the two are mixed in large quantities. Don't try it yourself, though ...

DID YOU KNOW?

Gold is the softest metal—a traditional test was to bite it and see if the teeth left a mark.

Shocking Science

WHAT IS THE BIGGEST THING IN EXISTENCE?
A massive supercluster of galaxies called the Hercules-Corona Borealis Great Wall is the biggest thing in existence. It is thought to be about 10 billion light-years in length.

WHAT ARE THE SMALLEST THINGS IN EXISTENCE?
The smallest things are called subatomic particles. There are various types, such as quarks, neutrinos, photons, and leptons.

HOW FAST IS THE EARTH?
The Earth is moving through space at an astonishing 107,000 km/h (66,487 mph)!

WHAT ARE THE BIGGEST STARS IN THE GALAXY?
The biggest stars in the galaxy are called supergiants and hypergiants. A red supergiant can be 1,500 times bigger than the Sun!

Shocking Science

HOW SMALL ARE ATOMS?
Atoms are particles so tiny that 4 billion would fit on the dot at the end of this sentence.

WHAT IS THE FASTEST THING IN THE UNIVERSE?
Light is the fastest thing in the universe. It travels at more than 300,000 km/h (180,000 mph).

DID YOU KNOW?
A total solar eclipse can be seen from the same place only once every 375 years.

CAN WATER CUT THROUGH METAL?
Water can cut through steel! Waterjet tools shoot water through a fine nozzle at such a high pressure that the jet cuts metal—and it never needs sharpening.

Shocking Science

DID YOU KNOW?
The 10 highest mountains in the world are all in the Himalayas.

WHO INVENTED EARMUFFS?
Earmuffs were invented by a 15-year-old American boy in the 19th century!

CAN A FISH SURVIVE OUT OF WATER?
A lungfish can live out of water for up to four years! During dry seasons, it burrows into mud and breathes through a pair of basic lungs.

DID YOU KNOW?
Oak trees don't produce acorns until they are 50 years old.

Shocking Science

DID YOU KNOW?

Under certain conditions, hot water freezes faster than cold water! This surprising phenomenon is called it the Mpemba effect, and has puzzled scientists for hundreds of years.

WHERE WERE THE FIRST TRAFFIC SIGNALS USED?

The first traffic signals were manually operated red and green gaslights placed outside London's Houses of Parliament. Unfortunately, they exploded and injured the police officer who was operating them.

WHAT IS SAND MADE OF?

Sand is mostly made from tiny pieces of the mineral quartz.

HOW MUCH DOES A CLOUD WEIGH?

They may look like cotton puffs, but clouds are made up of tiny water droplets with about one marble-sized amount of water for every 1 cubic m (35 cubic ft) of air, but it all adds up. An average cloud, about 1 cubic km (0.24 cubic mi) in volume, weighs more than 500 metric tons (551 tons)!

Shocking Science

CAN YOU RUN CARS ON SUGAR?
Yes. In parts of India, Brazil, and the USA, car fuel can be made from sugar!

CAN YOU BE STRUCK BY LIGHTNING WHILE INDOORS?
Yes! A bolt can travel down phone lines, electric cables, and plumbing pipes, so keep away from them during an electrical storm.

DID YOU KNOW?
The leaf of the giant Amazon water lily is so strong that you could sit on it without sinking!

WHERE IS THE WORLD'S TALLEST VOLCANO?
The largest volcano is Mauna Kea in Hawaii. It's 4,170 m (13,678 ft) tall, though most of it is hidden under the sea.

Shocking Science

WHOSE RAINCOATS WERE STINKY?

The first raincoats, designed by Charles Macintosh, were made waterproof with rubber and a by-product of coal tar. They kept people dry, but the smell was horrid!

WHAT CLASS EXPERIMENT WILL TAKE A HUNDRED YEARS TO END?

In 1930, a University of Queensland professor began an experiment with a funnel full of pitch (tar) to show his students how something that appears solid can be a liquid. The first drip took 10 years to fall, and the eighth drip fell in 2000. It will be a hundred years before all the pitch has dripped through, finishing the long, long experiment!

WHERE WAS THE FIRST HYDROELECTRIC POWER PLANT?

The world's first hydroelectric power plant used water from a lake to light a country house in Northumberland, England, in 1870.

Daring Deeds

CAN YOU SURF ON A RIVER?

Rivers don't usually produce waves for surfers to ride, but a natural event called a tidal bore can deliver the goods. These bizarre waves sweep down rivers at speeds of up to 40 km/h (25 mph) and can measure up to 9 m (30 ft) in height. They can also cover distances of up to 300 km (186 mi), if you can stay upright on your board that long.

WHERE IS THE MOST DANGEROUS BORE?

The Qiantang River tidal bore in China (known by locals as the "Silver Dragon") is the most notorious in the world.

DID YOU KNOW?

Tidal bores are known as "pororocas" in Brazil, which translates as "roar" or "destroyer." The name is apt, since surfing such unpredictable waves is fraught with physical danger. Many people have been injured while attempting to ride their way to fame and glory.

WHAT'S THE RECORD FOR SURFING A TIDAL BORE?

The longest nonstop tidal bore surfing record was set by Australian James Cotton in 2016 when he surfed the Kampar River in Sumatra, Indonesia. He managed to surf for 17.2 km (10.6 mi).

DID YOU KNOW?

Attempting to jump over Niagara Falls is illegal. Several people have been drowned or injured doing so—so it might be a good idea to rethink that world record plan!

Daring Deeds

IS THERE A REAL SPIDER-MAN?

A real-life daredevil has claimed the name "French Spider-Man" by scaling some of the world's tallest buildings without ropes or safety gear. Alain Roberts has been climbing unaided since he was a child—aged 12, he ascended eight floors of the apartment building where he lived because he had forgotten his keys. Roberts has since earned a world record for climbing the 300 m (984 ft)-high Aspire Tower in Qatar in 1 hour, 33 minutes, and 47 seconds.

WHICH BUILDINGS HAS THE FRENCH SPIDER-MAN CLIMBED?

Alain Roberts has reached the top of over 150 buildings over the years. These include the Empire State Building, New York; Canary Wharf, London; Eiffel Tower, Paris; Petronas Towers, Kuala Lumpur; Willis Tower, Chicago; and the world's tallest building, the 828 m (2,717 ft)-tall Burj Khalifa, Dubai.

IS IT LEGAL TO CLIMB PUBLIC BUILDINGS?

No, though Roberts sometimes gets official approval. He only managed to climb 2 m (6.5 ft) of the One Houston Center in Houston, Texas, USA, before he was arrested by the police! He has been arrested on several different occasions because of his climbing.

Daring Deeds

IS SOLO CLIMBING DANGEROUS?

Very! Alain Roberts puts his life at risk every time he attempts a climb. After falling 15 m (49 ft) headfirst in 1982, he was left in a coma for five days with fractures of the pelvis, elbows, heels, nose, and cranium. Fortunately, he recovered—and that painful experience hasn't put him off climbing at all!

HOW FAR CAN A BUS JUMP?

Don't ask the driver of your school bus to attempt this. Hollywood stuntman Steve Hudis pulled off the world record for the longest bus jump, taking the vehicle on a 33 m (108 ft) leap over 15 motorcycles while surrounded by a fireball!

DID YOU KNOW?

The original and greatest daredevil, Evel Knievel, would have approved of Hudis's stunt—but Knievel usually jumped buses on a bike, not the other way around!

Daring Deeds

WHERE CAN YOU SEE THE MOST DARING PILOTS IN ACTION?

Hurtling over land or water in a plane at breakneck speed, only 4.5 m (15 ft) from the surface, is risky. Now add an aerial racetrack marked by air-filled pylons to navigate, and you have the Red Bull Air Race World Championship. Between 2003 and 2019, this contest showcased the world's best pilots racing each other across international cities to win nothing more than prestige. Strapped into planes that can reach up to 370 km/h (229 mph), they raced around 5 km (3 mile)-long tracks, pulling the kind of turns that increases the pilot's body by a g-force of 12. The Red Bull event stopped in 2019, but in 2022 the event experienced a resurgence under a new organization, the Air Race World Championship.

WHAT IF A PLANE HIT A MAST DURING THE RED BULL RACE?

If the pilot clipped one of the masts in a dangerous move, then they can faced disqualification. The air-filled masts were designed to be as safe as possible when hit—which was frequently! Amazingly, when a plane's wing hit the top of a mast, it simply sliced through it like butter. The ground crew then rushed out and fix the mast, filling it back up with air in time for the next race.

HOW FAR CAN YOU TRAVEL ON A POGO STICK?

The distance to beat is 42.16 km (26.2 mi), a record set by Jack Sexty of the UK in 2014.

Daring Deeds

HOW FAR CAN YOU MOTORCYCLE BACKWARD?

The longest ever backward motorcycle journey was completed by Indian motorcycle stuntman Dipayan Choudhury, who rode his bike facing the wrong way for 202 km (126 mi).

WHAT'S THE RISKIEST STUNT THE DANGEROUS SPORTS CLUB ATTEMPTED?

In 2000, daredevil Stella Young was launched 21 m (69 ft) into the air with a medieval-style catapult. She soared through the air at 80 km/h (50 mph) before coming back down to Earth. When she hit the safety net, she bounced out and fell to the ground, fracturing her pelvis. Don't try this at home!

IS THERE A CLUB FOR DANGEROUS SPORTS?

The Dangerous Sports Club started in the UK in the late 1970s. They were the first to try the modern bungee jump; to hang glide off Mount Kilimanjaro; to sail across the English Channel tucked into the pouch of an inflatable kangaroo; and to fly around London's Big Ben in a microlight while dressed as a gorilla playing the saxophone. The group became infamous in the 1980s, since they would frequently find themselves either being arrested or challenged by officials—such as when they turned up at the Swiss ski resort of St. Moritz in a double-decker bus, ready to "drive" down the ski slope.

Daring Deeds

WHERE CAN YOU JOIN A STAMPEDE FOR FUN?

Every July, in the Spanish city of Pamplona, a herd of bulls is released to chase a reckless crowd through the streets. The running of the bulls is part of the Festival of San Fermin. This controversial custom sees everyone dressed in white with red neckerchiefs trying to outrun six fighting bulls, plus two herds of bullocks, along a 875 m (2,870 ft)-long course.

ARE PEOPLE HURT DURING THE RUNNING OF THE BULLS?

Yes. It may only take three minutes to complete the race, but every year multiple competitors are injured. Weirdly, that doesn't stop people from wanting to compete the next year! There is a gap between the two fences where medical teams stand, ready to rescue any participant who gets down by one of the bulls.

WHO WENT JUMPING ROPE WITH A TIGER?

American Ashrita Furman broke the fastest jump rope record by jumping rope 5 km (3 mi) in 35 minutes, 19 seconds. He skipped at Tiger Temple in Thailand, and had a tiger for company, trotting alongside him most of the way!

Daring Deeds

HOW FAST CAN YOU RIDE ON A MOUNTAIN BIKE?

To reach the fastest speeds, you'll need a steep slope, no obstacles, and a serious disregard for your own safety! Austrian daredevil Markus Stöckl, known as "Hercules," smashed the world speed record for series mountain bikes by shooting down the snow-covered, 45-degree, 2000 m (6,562 ft)-long LaParva slope in Chile, hitting a top speed of 338.7 km/h (210.4 mph).

WHAT IS THE COOLEST WAY TO FLY?

How about your own personal jet wing? It may sound like something out of a James Bond movie, but the jet wing is the real deal. Featuring four separate jet engines, it was built by Swiss pilot Yves Rossy in his garage. The personal flying machine has been used to fly over the Grand Canyon, across the English Channel, and over the Alps.

WHAT KIND OF PERSON WANTS TO FLY A JET WING?

Yves Rossy is a true daredevil. When not breaking records with his jet-powered wing, Yves used to fly Mirage fighters for the Swiss army and is now an airline pilot. In his downtime, he likes to parachute—he's done over 1,100 jumps!

WHY DID HERCULES HAVE TO HOLD HIS BREATH?

It took Markus "Hercules" Stoeckl only 40 seconds to complete his record-breaking, high-speed run, which was lucky. He had to hold his breath while breaking the record, or else his special aerodynamic helmet would have steamed up due to his warm breath!

Daring Deeds

WHAT'S THE HEAVIEST THING YOU CAN SWALLOW?

British man Thomas Blackthorne is a man of many bizarre hobbies—he eats glass, shampoo, and razor blades and enjoys sleeping in pits of snakes. He's also partial to walking on sword blades and through acid baths. But perhaps his most spectacular feat was lowering the 24 mm (1 in)-long bit of a demolition hammer into his throat and holding it—and the entire weight of the hammer—for three seconds. The hammer weighed 38 kg (84 lb), about half the weight of a grown man, and had to be hoisted up via a motorized chain.

HOW MUCH PASTA CAN YOU LIFT?

Blackthorne also set a record for the heaviest tongue lift when he picked up 12.5 kg (27 lb) of pasta in a glass-walled box using just his tongue.

CAN DOGS SKYDIVE?

Yes! Specially trained dogs that work with U.S. Navy SEALS wear a canine tandem skydiving harness, so they can be strapped to their handlers and parachuted into combat situations.

Daring Deeds

WHO IS THE HUMAN FIREBALL?

Austrian firefighter Josef Tödtling has little fear of flames. He set the record for the longest full-body burn without an oxygen supply in 2013. He managed to stay alight (and alive) for 5 minutes and 41 seconds. His body was protected by multiple layers of clothing and a cooling gel.

HOW FAR CAN YOU BICYCLE WITHOUT USING YOUR HANDS?

American bicyclist Erik Skamstad bicycled 37 km 417 m (23.25 mi) around the Las Vegas Motor Speedway—without using his hands.

DID YOU KNOW?

The record number of spoons one person has balanced on parts of their body is 88.

CAN KIDS TAME LIONS?

It's an odd hobby for a kid, but Spain's Jorge Elich is the world's youngest lion tamer. The youngest in a family of six brothers and sisters, he started taming lions when he was just five years old, helping out his lion-taming dad.

Daring Deeds

DID YOU KNOW?

Parachutes have a hole in the top! The modern design lets built-up air through, which in old parachutes used to cause a swinging motion.

CAN YOU SURVIVE A JUMP FROM A PLANE WITHOUT A PARACHUTE?

US stuntman Travis Pastrana enjoys skydiving—without a parachute! In one hair-raising stunt, he leaped from a plane 3,810 m (12,500 ft) in the air without one and had to glide his way to his jump partner, who grabbed his hands. This allowed Travis to pull himself onto his fellow skydiver's back before his partner's parachute cord was pulled.

HOW MANY TIMES CAN YOU FLIP OVER A MOTORCYCLE?

How about twice, backward? Motocross legend Travis Pastrana managed to perform the world's first freestyle motocross double backflip in the fearsome X Games. The amazing feat also landed him the highest score ever given by the judges at the Best Trick event. Travis rehearsed his double backflip over 1,000 times in a special foam pit he has at home.

HOW MANY MAGIC TRICKS CAN YOU PERFORM UNDERWATER IN A MINUTE?

A teenaged girl named Avery Emerson Fisher performed 38 magic tricks in one minute while scuba diving at an aquarium in San Francisco.

Daring Deeds

HOW LONG COULD YOU STAY UNDERWATER?

American Richard Presley lived in an underwater module for 69 days and 19 minutes as part of research into the effects of living under the sea.

WHAT COOL STUNTS CAN YOU DO IN A WHEELCHAIR?

As a teenager, Aaron "Wheels" Fotheringham gained fame for the extreme stunts he pulled in his wheelchair at a skateboard park in California, USA. He landed himself a world record for performing the first-ever backflip in a wheelchair. His chair was made from tough, light metal, had special suspension to cope with the impact of landings, and featured "grind bars" that helped Aaron achieve his amazing stunts.

WHO SURVIVED THE MOST CRASHES?

As part of his job, American W. R. "Rusty" Haight was a human crash-test dummy who recorded more than 1,000 collisions.

Daring Deeds

COULD YOU SURVIVE BEING BURIED ALIVE?

Geoff Smith of Mansfield, UK, was buried under the yard of a pub in a 2.1 m (6.8 ft)-long wooden box. He stayed down there for a record-breaking 147 days, breathing through a tube that was also used to pass food down to him and for the removal of body waste. For company, Geoff had a small television, a personal stereo, a phone, and a tiny Christmas tree, since he ended up spending Christmas buried alive as well! Geoff buried himself in tribute to his late mother, who had set the original world record of 101 days.

HOW LONG CAN YOU STAY UNDERGROUND WITHOUT FOOD AND WATER?

The record for the most time spent buried alive without food or water belongs to Zdenek Zahradka, who spent 10 days in 2004 buried in a coffin in Jaromer, Czech Republic.

CAN YOU SNOWBOARD IN A CAR?

Well, no, but that doesn't stop anyone from trying to copy the moves. Successful rally driver Ken Block loves to go jumping in his rally car, and he has jumped 52 m (171 ft) for a TV show, reaching 7.6 m (25 ft) in the air. But his most incredible achievement was the astonishing jump he did halfway up a snow-covered mountain in 2007. Ken headed to New Zealand's Snow Park in his specially equipped car, then made a huge jump in sync with a pro snowboarder, showcasing his signature style of blending motorsports with snowboarding.

Daring Deeds

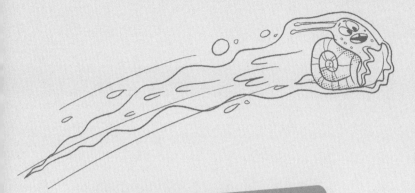

WHO ELSE WAS BURIED ALIVE FOR A STUNT?

In 2008, performer David Blaine was buried alive for seven days in a transparent box under a 3 metric ton (3.3 ton) water tank in New York City. He had no food and hardly any water.

HOW FAR CAN YOU SPIT A SNAIL?

Snail-spitting champion Alain Jourden can spit a snail 9.4 m (31 ft). Competitors take a running start before they spit out their slimy bug as far as they can.

CAN YOU WALK A HIGHLINE ACROSS A VOLCANO?

In December 2022, Matías Grez set a record for walking a highline across the world's highest volcano, Nevada Ojos del Salado on the Chile-Argentina border in South America. The highline was 33 m (110 ft) long and at an elevation of 6,880 m (22,572 ft).

WHO BUILT A TOWER MADE OF HAM?

Artist Gayle Chong Kwan has made sculptured landscapes from food. Her works have included puffed rice walls, mashed potato mountains, cheese buildings, and a ham tower.

FABULOUS FACTS

Fabulous Facts

WHAT IS THE WORLD'S BIGGEST BOARD GAME?

How about playing Monopoly where you are the game piece? A massive Monopoly board displayed at the Sydney Home Show in Australia measured a massive 440 sq m (4,736 sq ft), earning it the world record for being the biggest of its type. The hotels and houses, which make up a key part of the game, were a whopping 1,700 times larger than the ones used in the regular board game.

COULD YOU PLAY IT?

No, but there is another, slightly smaller version you can enjoy at Monopoly in the Park in San Jose, California, USA. There, you'll find an 86 sq m (926 sq ft) outdoor board (officially the largest outdoor version of Monopoly in the world) for rent. Expect to wear huge token-shaped hats, play with massive dice, and to put on a prison outfit if you're sent to jail.

WHAT IS THE TINIEST CHILDREN'S BOOK?

Teeny Ted from Turnip Town is a children's book written by Malcolm Douglas Chaplin. You can't see it with the human eye. To read it, you need an electron microscope. It's 0.07 x 0.1 mm (0.003 x 0.004 in) and is made up of 30 carved tablets placed side by side. Its creators, Karen Kavanagh and Li Yang, hoped to publish more than one copy, though buyers would need to spend around £14,400 (about $18,475) for the microscopic title.

Fabulous Facts

HOW LONG CAN BOARD GAMES LAST?

The longest recorded game of Monopoly took a wearisome 70 days to complete—nonstop! As for other board games, the record for playing board games in a treehouse is 286 hours—almost 12 days. And playing upside down? Well, 26 hours is the time to beat!

WHAT IS THE SMALLEST BOOK YOU CAN BUY?

Just the size of a match head, the world's smallest commercially produced book was published by German company Die Gestalten Verlag in 2002. The 2.4 x 2.9 mm (0.09 x 0.11 in) book was created by the typographer Josua Reichert and boasted 26 pages. The leather-bound title was delivered in a mahogany box along with a magnifying glass so you could read it. But the title was no murder mystery or fantasy. There was only space on each page of the book for one letter of the alphabet.

DID YOU KNOW?

Over 5 billion of the green houses that are featured in Monopoly have been made since the board game was first introduced in 1935.

DID YOU KNOW?

The world's longest hot dog measured an impressive 203.8 m (668 ft 8 in) long!

Fabulous Facts

WHERE IS THE LONGEST BRIDGE IN EUROPE?

The Vasco da Gama bridge is the longest bridge in the European Union at 12.3 km (7.6 mi) long. It was so vast that engineers had to take into account the curvature of the Earth! It cost £722 million (about $926 million) to build.

DID YOU KNOW?

Carhenge, located on the plains near Alliance, Nebraska, USA, is a replica of England's Stonehenge ... made with 39 vintage cars!

WHAT WAS THE BIGGEST DINNER PARTY?

Back in 1998, a record-breaking feast took place in Lisbon, Portugal, where a 5 km (3 mile)-long dining table was set up along the newly opened Vasco da Gama bridge to serve 16,000 people! Guests enjoyed a traditional Portuguese dish, the famous feijoada stew ... 10 metric tons (11 tons) of it! The event was organized by a dishwashing detergent manufacturer who claimed that the dirty dishes could all be cleaned using just 1 l (2.11 pt) of their dishwashing liquid. But who would volunteer to do the dishwashing?!

Fabulous Facts

WHAT IS THE WORLD'S MOST USELESS INVENTION?

There are lots of contenders for the title of most useless invention. The best person to judge is Kenji Kawakami, the creator of the Japanese practice of Chindogu, which loosely translated means "un-useless ideas." Among the inventions he has accepted are an outdoor toilet seat with a layer of artificial grass to keep your bottom warm and an alarm clock that has pins on the off button so you never need to worry about turning it off and falling back to sleep.

WHEN WAS THE FIRST CASH MACHINE INSTALLED?

The first cash machine was installed in a New York bank in 1939, but it was taken out six months later because customers didn't like it. No more were installed for 25 years after that!

WHAT MAKES AN INVENTION USELESS?

Kawakami has set a series of rules for Chindogu inventions:

1. A Chindogu cannot be for real use.
2. A Chindogu must exist.
3. Chindogu must represent freedom of thought and action.
4. Chindogu are tools for everyday life.
5. Chindogu are not for sale.
6. Comedy must not be the sole reason for creating Chindogu.
7. Chindogu are not propaganda.
8. Chindogu are never taboo.
9. Chindogu cannot be patented.
10. Chindogu are without prejudice.

DID YOU KNOW?

In the 1960s, an inventor in Japan came up with a cat meow machine to scare off rodents. The device meowed 10 times per minute, and the eyes lit up. Rats and mice weren't fooled, though, so it wasn't a big success.

Fabulous Facts

CAN YOU LIVE IN A TOILET?

If you must, there is a toilet-shaped house in South Korea, built in 2007 to mark the launch of the first meeting of the World Toilet Association. The 419 sq m (4,510 sq ft) building, made from steel, glass, and white concrete, boasts four deluxe toilets—some featuring electronic motion sensors that detect when your bottom is about to descend. You can rent the house for £36,000 (about $46,185) a day.

COULD YOU EAT A MILE-LONG DESSERT?

Never mind a mile, how about 8 km (5 mi) long? That's how long the world's longest banana split was. You might need to share it!

WHO IS MR. TOILET?

The toilet house was built by Sim Jae-duck, who is known in South Korea as "Mr. Toilet" because of his political work trying to turn public restrooms into pleasant places to visit. Indeed, the toilet-shaped house is called Haewoojae, which means "a place of sanctuary where one can solve one's worries."

HOW BIG IS THE WORLD'S BIGGEST ROLL OF TOILET PAPER?

The biggest roll of toilet paper was created by toilet paper company Charmin in 2011. It's an enormous 2.97 m (9 ft 9 in) in diameter.

Fabulous Facts

HOW MANY BLOCKS WERE USED IN THE WORLD'S LARGEST MINI BRICK BUILD?

The record number of LEGO bricks used was 150 million! Fifty designers in China assembled a scene from *The Lord of the Rings* over three years, completing it in 2024.

HOW MANY LEGO BRICKS WOULD IT TAKE TO REACH THE MOON?

If you could fit the bricks on top of each other in a long, straight tower, you would need 40,000,000,000 LEGO bricks to reach from the Earth to the Moon.

HOW TALL A TOWER CAN YOU BUILD FROM LEGO?

The tallest tower ever made out of LEGO bricks was built in Milan, Italy, in 2015, and measured an astonishing 35.05 m (114 ft 11 in). Roughly 550,000 plastic bricks were used to complete the tower, and the LEGO group donated €7 (about £6/$8) to an environmental charity for every 1 cm (0.4 in) built.

Fabulous Facts

WHO IS THE WEIRDEST CYCLING FAN?

One character who could claim that title is German cycling enthusiast Dieter "Didi" Senft. He is often seen by the road during the Tour de France, jumping up and down in his signature devil costume. Sporting red Lycra and horns, he keeps the riders entertained. He's been turning up at the competition as the devil since 1993 and paints a devil's pitchfork on the road miles before he makes his appearance, so the riders have fair warning.

WHERE CAN YOU FIND THE WORLD'S WEIRDEST BICYCLE?

"Didi" Senft also builds bizarre bikes. One of his wild creations is the world's biggest mobile guitar, a 500 kg (1,102 lb) guitar-shaped bicycle. It took Didi six months to create, and the end result is 40 m (131 ft) long and 4.2 m (13.8 ft) high. Because of the guitar bike's extreme length, Didi is not allowed to ride it on public roads.

CAN YOU DRIVE A HAMBURGER?

Yes! Sudhakar Yadav is famous for his wacky vehicle designs. Along with a hamburger, Yadav has designed cars and bikes to look like a racing helmet, a coffee mug, and a camera. In total, he has created over 200 bizarre vehicles. Based in India, Yadav is a huge cricket fan and even built a 7.5 m (24.6 ft)-long cricket bat car to go with his vehicles based on sports equipment such as a basketball, football, and tennis ball.

131

Fabulous Facts

CAN YOU DRIVE A TOILET?
Sudhakar Yadav also designed a toilet-shaped car featuring a 50 cc engine and boasting a top speed of 40 km/h (25 mph). The driver sits in the bowl with the lid up. It is not clear if Yadav fitted a working flush lever, though.

WHICH ADDRESS HAS SIX POSTAL CODES?
The Pentagon, headquarters of the United States Department of Defense in Washington, D.C., is the world's biggest office building and has six postcodes (zip codes) all to itself.

DID YOU KNOW?
The highest internet café in the world is at Mount Everest base camp, more than 5,000 m (16,404 ft) above sea level.

WHOSE ARTWORK CAN CAUSE A STINK?
College lecturer Paul Rogerson creates award-winning sculptures ... from lard! His works of characters from Bugs Bunny to Don Quixote last only two months before they start to become a bit stinky.

Fabulous Facts

WHERE IS THE LONGEST SWIMMING POOL IN THE WORLD?

You'd better be prepared if you're off to the Chilean resort of San Alfonso del Mar, because swimming just a single length of its pool means a 1 km (0.6 mi) splash. The world's largest pool took five years to build and cost £1 billion (about $1.3 billion). It features a 35 m (115 ft) deep end—about eight times taller than your average three-bedroom house! The water remains so clear at the deep end that you can still see the bottom.

HOW LONG DOES IT TAKE TO BUILD A SPACE STATION?

It took 10 years and more than 30 space missions to build the International Space Station.

HOW MUCH WATER IS IN THE WORLD'S BIGGEST SWIMMING POOL?

It took 2.5 million l (550,000 gal) of seawater to fill the pool, which is kept clean in an environmentally friendly way. For those of you who feel too weary to doggy paddle across, kayaks and sailboats are on hand to whisk guests around. The huge pool is equivalent to 6,000 standard swimming pools.

WAS ANOTHER TITANIC EVER BUILT?

The sister ship of RMS *Titanic* was to be named *Gigantic*, but its name was changed to *Britannic* after the disaster involving the first ship. *Britannic* sunk, too, after hitting a mine in 1916.

Fabulous Facts

WHAT IS A MONOWHEEL?

Imagine a large wheel with an engine inside and space for you to sit. This is a monowheel, a design first proposed in the late 19th century and now something of a curiosity. The quirky vehicle became an obsession for Kerry McLean of Michigan, USA. His top-of-the-range monowheel was fitted with a Buick V8 engine and managed speeds of 86 km (54 mi) per hour. Known as the Rocket Roadster, McLean set the world land speed record for powered single-wheelers at the Bonneville Salt Flats in Utah, USA.

WHERE IS THE MOST TOPSY-TURVY PLACE IN THE WORLD?

If you decide to pay a visit to the remarkable upside-down house on the German island of Usedom, don't try to use the restroom. Everything inside the structure is also upside down! That includes the chairs, carpets, and toilets. The house has become something of a hit with tourists because they enter via the attic and then navigate their way round the 120 sq m (1,292 sq ft) family-sized home.

CAN A BUILDING MAKE YOU FEEL UNWELL?

Another upside-down house, in Poland, has proved so popular that visitors have been known to line up for up to six hours to get inside. But there are reports that visitors can end up feeling seasick. The builders who constructed the house had to take regular breaks because of feeling disoriented—so the house ended up taking five times longer to build than a normal house.

Fabulous Facts

WHERE IS THE WORLD'S BIGGEST AQUARIUM?

The world's biggest aquarium opened in 2005 in Atlanta, Georgia, USA. The Georgia Aquarium contains more than 100,000 sea creatures.

WHICH SPANISH BUILDING HAS BEEN UNDERWAY FOR OVER 100 YEARS?

Construction of Barcelona's unique Sagrada Familia cathedral began in 1883, and it still isn't finished! Work is due to be completed in 2026.

DID YOU KNOW?

The Eiffel Tower sways up to 7 cm (almost 3 in) in the wind.

WHAT IS THE MOST POPULAR MONUMENT IN THE WORLD?

Almost 300 million people, an average of 7 million a year, have visited Paris's Eiffel Tower since it was built, making it the world's most visited monument.

Fabulous Facts

WHAT IS THE HEAVIEST OBJECT EVER WEIGHED?

The heaviest object ever weighed was a launchpad, Revolving Service Structure (RSS), at NASA's Kennedy Space Center in Florida, USA. The RSS weighed 2,423 metric tons (2,672 tons).

CAN YOU RIDE A SHOPPING CART ON THE ROAD?

New Zealand's Duncan Everson attached a moped engine to the underbody of a cart, fitted it with the wheels from a lawn mower, and has since been motoring around the roads of Palmerston North, New Zealand. It boasts 50 cc of power, can go up to 45 km/h (28 mph), and is totally road legal. But what does he put his shopping in?

DID YOU KNOW?

The largest toothpick sculpture was named Alligator Alley. It was made by American Michael Smith from more than 3 million toothpicks!

Fabulous Facts

WHO BUILT A TORNADO-PROOF CAR?

Most people stay as far away as possible from tornados, but cinematographer Sean Casey wanted to sit inside one. He built a tough, metal-plated Tornado Intercept Vehicle, so he could film a direct hit from a tornado and record its speed.

DID YOU KNOW?

Architecture was once an Olympic sport! Along with other arts, it was considered an essential part of the famous Games.

CAN YOU TURN A STONE COLLECTION INTO A PALACE?

Yes! A mailman in France spent 33 years collecting a special type of stone while he was out on his rounds. He used the stones to build the fanciful Le Palais Idéal, which is now a designated cultural landmark.

HOW WAS THE MICROWAVE OVEN INVENTED?

American engineer Percy Spencer invented the microwave oven after a chocolate bar melted in his pocket as he stood next to a radar tube.

FREAKY FEATS

Freaky Feats

WHAT DOES MONSIEUR MANGETOUT EAT?

Dubbed "Monsieur Mangetout," Michel Lotito shocked people with his unorthodox appetite for anything that didn't contain vitamins—including 18 bicycles, seven televisions, two beds, and an entire coffin. His amazing ability to chow down on up to 900 g (2 lb) of metal every day was the result of his stomach lining being twice the thickness of a normal person's and constant practice from the age of nine.

HOW MANY HOTDOGS IS TOO MANY?

You'll need an awesome appetite to compete at Nathan's Famous July Fourth International Hot Dog Eating Contest in New York. A regular world-beater, Joey Chestnut, has been munching his way across the USA and holds several records for his eating antics—in this particular case, consuming 76 hotdogs in less than 10 minutes in 2021.

CAN YOU EAT A PLANE?

It's not your average airline meal. Over two years, feasting Frenchman Michel Lotito ate his way through a Cessna 150 aircraft. It was a stunt that earned him not only a world record but also brought him to the attention of the world's media.

Freaky Feats

CAN YOU WIN AT EATING BREAKFAST?

For the greediest and speediest, London, UK, has an annual All You Can Eat Breakfast Eating Championship. To be in with a chance of winning, you need to beat the record of Luppan Yau, who managed to polish off five-and-a-half breakfasts—egg, bacon, sausage, mushrooms, and croissant—in an amazing 12 minutes. He had previously set a record for eating the most doughnuts in three minutes.

WHO TOOK THE FIRST HOT-AIR BALLOON FLIGHT?

The first living creatures to go up in a hot-air balloon, in 1783, were a sheep, a duck, and a rooster.

WHO IS THE PIERCING HEAVYWEIGHT?

Brazilian-born Elaine Davidson is a world record holder for being the most pierced woman on the planet. The former nurse, who now lives in Edinburgh, UK, was first spotted when she sported 462 piercings (with 192 of those being on her face). She now has over 6,000!

WHO DELIVERED THE MOST PIERCINGS AT ONE TIME?

UK-based Charlie Wilson and Kam Ma took up the uncomfortable challenge of speed-piercing in 2006, with a record 1,015 piercings made over seven hours and 55 minutes.

Freaky Feats

WHO HAS THE BIGGEST MOUTH?
Italian Francisco Domingos Joaquim boasts the biggest mouth in the world, stretching to 17 cm (6.69 in) wide.

WHO WAS THE TALLEST MAN RECORDED?
The tallest man ever to have lived was American Robert Wadlow. By the time he died in 1940, Robert measured an astonishing 2.72 m (8 ft 11 in).

HOW DO YOU HELP A GIANT FIND LOVE?
Measuring in at a towering 2.3 m (7 ft 9 in), Mongolian Bao Xishun was, for a while, the world's tallest man. Though in good health, he found it difficult to find love. An international appeal was set up to find him a suitable bride before he met a saleswoman from his hometown, Chifeng. They tied the knot and became the proud parents of an only slightly bigger-than-average son.

WHO IS THE WORLD'S HEAVIEST MAN?
At his peak, American Jon Brower Minnoch weighed over 635 kg (1,400 lb). He was so heavy that he was confined to his bed for a lot of his life. After several health problems, he lost a whopping 419 kg (924 lb).

Freaky Feats

WHO WAS THE TREE MAN OF JAVA?

It began with a single small wart on Dede Koswara's lower leg when he was 15 years old. Then the wart spread all over his body. By the time the man from West Java, Indonesia, came to the attention of the media, his hands and feet were covered in huge clumps of warts that looked like tree bark. After becoming known as "The Tree Man of Java," experts discovered that he had a rare condition that kept his body from fighting off warts. The bizarre growths are known as "cutaneous horns."

WAS THE TREE MAN OF JAVA CURED?

Surgeons performed several operations on Dede Koswara to remove his growths—one operation saw them remove a staggering 2 kg (4.4 lb) of warts from his hands and feet. Thanks to the operations, Dede was able to use his hands again for the first time in over 10 years.

WHO WAS THE QUEEN OF CORSETS?

American woman Cathie Jung is famous for having the world's smallest waist, measuring a teeny tiny 38.1 cm (15 in). Cathie pulled this off by wearing corsets pulled very tightly day and night for over 25 years. Cathie is married to an orthopedic surgeon, who believes Cathie's love of corset wearing does her no harm and could actually help support her spine, not damage it.

WHO WAS THE SHORTEST MAN RECORDED?

The world's shortest human adult ever verified was Chandra Bahadur Dangi of Nepal. He measured just 54.6 cm (21.5 in).

Freaky Feats

WHO HAS THE WORLD'S BIGGEST TONGUE?

Nick Stoeberl of the USA has a record-breaking tongue that measures 10.1 cm (3.97 in) from its tip to the middle of his closed lips. How does he fit that in his mouth?

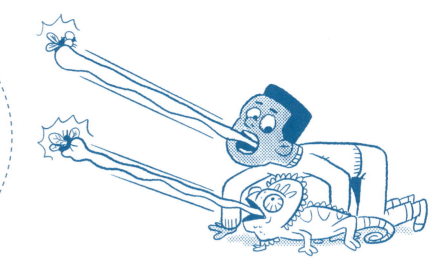

WHO USED HIS TEETH TO STOP A PLANE TAKING OFF?

Georges Christen is a mountain of muscle. He's bent 269 nails in an hour, pulled a 22- (24-ton) rail car 100 m (328 ft), and much more. Perhaps his most impressive feat was when he kept three Cessna aircraft from taking off, using his arms to stop two of them from moving and using his teeth to stop the third. It's all the more impressive because the planes' engines were cranked up to full power at the time!

CAN YOU BURST A HOT-WATER BOTTLE WITH YOUR BREATH?

Superstrong Christen also enjoys blowing up ho -water bottles—it takes him 40 seconds to inflate one with his breath before it pops. He has to be extremely careful, though, because if he allowed the air to rush back into his lungs, his lungs would explode!

DID YOU KNOW?

The longest cuddle ever lasted for 5,000 years! Archaeologists discovered a pair of entwined skeletons in Northern Italy and believe the couple to be from the Neolithic period.

Freaky Feats

WHO EATS THE MOST ICE CREAM?

The world's leading ice cream eaters are the Australians, scoffing 16.6 l (4.3 gallons) per person each year.

CAN YOU ROLLER-SKATE UNDER A CAR?

At the age of seven, Aniket Chindak from India was already an ace on roller skates. But his top talent was skating while doing the splits, leaning over to hold onto his toes. When limbo-skating, Aniket's body is never more than 20 cm (8 in) above the ground. After training for up to four hours a day, sometimes skating as much as 97 km (60 mi) in a single week, Aniket managed to limbo-skate under 82 cars in just 53 seconds.

WHERE MIGHT YOU FIND THE WORLD'S HAIRIEST FAMILY?

The Gomez family from Mexico suffer from a condition known as "hypertrichosis," which means that they have thick hair all over their bodies. Danny Ramos Gomez performs as an acrobat alongside his brother, Larry, for the National Circus. Because of their condition, they had a difficult start in life—they spent their childhood in a freak show where they were named the "wolf children" and laughed at by passersby. Thankfully, they were rescued by the son of a circus owner and have been trained in many different performing arts.

Freaky Feats

CAN YOU SURVIVE FOR AN HOUR IN ICE?

Wim Hof, aka the Ice Man, is a Dutchman able to withstand the kind of temperatures that would prove fatal for the rest of us. Among his chilly records are swimming for over 57 m (187 ft) under ice, the fastest half marathon run barefoot over snow, and 1 hour 42 minutes of full body contact with ice. Wim reckons that his ability to withstand such extreme icy conditions is down to a Himalayan meditation technique, which he claims can generate heat in any part of his body.

WHOSE LEGS ARE LEGENDARY?

Russian supermodel and basketball player Ekaterina Lisina holds the record for the longest legs of any woman in the world at 132.8 cm (52 in). Not only is she the world's tallest professional model, Ekaterina, who is 205.7 cm (6ft 9in) tall, won a bronze Olympic medal as part of the Russian basketball team in 2008.

WHO'S TOP OF THE BELLY FLOPPERS?

Darren Taylor, aka Professor Splash, from Denver, Colorado, USA, regularly sets world records for the highest shallow diving. One record-breaking feat saw him dive from 10.7 m (35 ft) into a mere 30.5 cm (12 in) of water.

HOW MANY PEOPLE HAVE TWERKED AT ONE TIME?

The record for the greatest number of people twerking simultanously is 406. The record was set In New York in 2013.

Freaky Feats

DID YOU KNOW?
The youngest person to visit the undersea wreck of the *Titanic* was 13-year-old Sebastian Harris in 2005.

WHO CHANGED HIS APPEARANCE TO LOOK LIKE A TIGER?

Feline fan Dennis "Stalking Cat" Avner went to town in an effort to look more catlike. He had surgery to flatten and upturn his nose, had his teeth removed and tigerlike fangs inserted in their place, had brow implants fitted, and had his body covered in striped tiger tattoos. He even had his ears lengthened! On top of all that, Dennis has also had receptacles fitted to his upper lip, which means he can attach whiskers on special occasions. He is officially the world's most modified man.

WHO ARRANGED A DATE IN A GRAVE?

A middle-aged Chinese bachelor placed an ad asking for someone to share his grave—so he wouldn't be lonely in the afterlife! It's not known if he got a reply.

HOW MANY PEGS CAN YOU ATTACH TO YOUR FACE?

For stretchy-skinned Kelvin Mercado, the answer is a staggering 163. Don't even think about trying to beat that!

Freaky Feats

HOW DO YOU PLAY AN INVISIBLE GUITAR?

You don't need a guitar to be a guitar hero. In the Air Guitar World Championships held in Finland each year, competitors show off their air-guitar skills to two 60-second songs. Using only body movement and ludicrous facial expressions, they mimic an amazing guitar performance. No real instruments are allowed, although you can use a plectrum (pick).

DID YOU KNOW?

Bao Xishun, the world's tallest man at the time, saved the lives of two dolphins in 2006 by reaching into their stomachs with his 1.06 m (3.48 ft)-long arms and removing pieces of plastic.

WHAT DO GOATEE, CHINESE, MUSKETEER, AND IMPERIAL HAVE IN COMMON?

These are all styles of beard. The World Beard and Moustache Championships has three main categories: Moustache (Mustache), Partial Beard, and Full Beard. Within these, there are classes, including natural goatee, Chinese, Musketeer, Imperial, Partial Beard Freestyle, and the dramatic Sideburns Freestyle class. The Freestyle classes are the most popular—one competitor at a Berlin event used his beard to recreate the city's famous Brandenburg Gate, which included horses and flags!

147

Freaky Feats

HOW MANY LANGUAGES CAN ONE PERSON SPEAK?

Liberian-born Ziad Fazah is believed to be the world's greatest living polyglot—meaning someone who speaks multiple languages. He claims to be able to communicate in 59 different languages, although he can only speak 15 of those languages fluently.

WHAT IS GURNING?

Gurning is the art of face pulling. One of the world's top gurners is Briton Tommy "Quasimodo" Mattinson, who has won the World Gurning Championship 17 times. Held at the Egremont Crab Fair in Cumbria, UK, the gurning championship is world-famous for featuring people putting their heads through a horse collar and proceeding to scrunch up their features into the most hideous poses imaginable.

DO WOMEN GURN?

Anne Woods' gurning was arguably even more impressive than Tommy's facial antics in recent events. She gurned "competitively" for over 30 years and won the Ladies' Gurning Championship a staggering 28 times. Anne's success could be attributed to her being able to remove her dentures, making it possible for her to squash her face into unusual and surprising shapes.

Freaky Feats

DID YOU KNOW?
Australian Marawa Ibrahim set the Hula-Hoop world record in 2015, with 200 hoops at once. See how many you can manage!

CAN YOU SURVIVE BEING FIRED FROM A CANNON?
Not only can you survive, you can make a living from it! The Smith family have been firing themselves out of cannons for decades. First was David "Cannonball" Smith Sr., who made his name by setting the world record for the farthest human cannonball flight at 56 m (184 ft) in 1998. Then, his son, David "The Bullet" Smith Jr., stepped in, followed by sister, Stephanie, and a cousin, Rebecca. David Jr. broke his dad's record in 2018, soaring 59 m (194 ft).

DOES IT HURT?
Being shot out of a cannonball at 120 km/h (75 mph) is no walk in the park. Being a human cannonball requires proper planning—calculations have to be made to ensure that you land in the safety net 45 m (148 ft) away and the wind, distance, and height must be considered. As you're fired out, you can expect to experience a force of 11 gs—that's about 11 times your body weight.

DID YOU KNOW?
The largest number of living creatures produced during a magic performance was 80,000 bees in a show by Las Vegas magicians Penn and Teller.

Freaky Feats

DO NINJAS EXIST?

While legendary ninja assassins may no longer exist, in the Japanese town of Iga, people celebrate ninjas with a five-week-long festival every April. People dressed as the deadly warriors perform dances, host martial arts competitions, and spend time perfecting their ninja star-throwing skills. Many of the 30,000 visitors come dressed for the part in stealth gear with swords, plus small ones for the kids.

WERE NINJAS REALLY DEADLY?

Yes. Ninjas were a mercenary bunch who would carry out all manner of murder, espionage, sabotage, and theft for the right price. Their incredible talent for using stealth, disguises, and deadly weaponry made them feared throughout Japan. A few hundred ninjas managed to wipe out 10,000 samurai in a fierce battle in 1580.

WHO OWNS THE MOST OWL TOYS?

Before his death, Israel's Yaakov Chai owned a collection of 19,100 owl-related items. After he passed away, his friends and family began adding more items to the collection, bringing it to a grand total of 20,239 owls!

Freaky Feats

WHO HAS THE BIGGEST COLLECTION OF JET FIGHTERS IN THE WORLD?

Forget air forces, we're talking private collectors here, and French winemaker Michel Pont is a world-beater. Since 1985, he has owned up to 110 jet fighters (real, not toys), which make him officially the biggest private collector of jet fighters in the world. The planes are kept on the site of his 40-acre vineyard in the Burgundy region of France. And should he get bored with looking over his aircraft collection, he can always take to the road on one of his 300 motorcycles or in one of his 34 race cars.

CAN HE FLY HIS JET FIGHTER COLLECTION?

No. Pont is unable to take off in any of the planes from his huge vineyard because the fighters are banned from use in French airspace!

WHERE ARE BABIES ENCOURAGED TO CRY?

At the annual Naki Sumo Crying Baby Festivals across Japan, crying is positively encouraged. Each baby is held by a student sumo wrestler, who coaxes the baby into howling by pulling scary faces. If this fails, the sumo wrestlers can resort to putting on their scary fighting masks. The baby who cries first is declared the winner.

HOW LOUD IS A BABY'S CRY?

A baby's crying can be as loud as 110 decibels—that's as loud as a power saw!

Freaky Feats

WHO EATS THE MOST BAKED BEANS?

Britons lead the world in baked-bean consumption! According to bean manufacturer Heinz, the UK eats more baked beans than the rest of the world combined—a lip-licking 444 million cans every year.

WHO GAVE A TOMATO A FUNERAL?

During its early years, tomato fighting was banned in Buñol, Spain. But in 1955, the locals decided that they wanted the event made official and voiced their protest over the ban. They marched through the streets to a funeral march while carrying a coffin containing a large tomato. The authorities relented, and La Tomatina was here to stay.

WHERE CAN YOU JOIN THE BIGGEST FOOD FIGHT?

The world's biggest food fight happens every year in Buñol, Spain. During the infamous La Tomatina, more than 40,000 people arm themselves with around 140 metric tons (155 tons) of tomatoes and start pelting each other with the fruity missiles for over two hours. Organizers claim that the tomato war started in August 1945 when a fight broke out during a festival, which grew to a full-blown food fight as they grabbed tomatoes from a market stall.

Freaky Feats

DID YOU KNOW?
You're more likely to remember your dreams if you have an interrupted night's sleep and are woken up multiple times.

WHERE IS THE BIGGEST WATER FIGHT IN THE WORLD?

Every year in April, Thai people take to the streets armed with water pistols, buckets of water, waterlogged sponges, and the odd elephant, to dowse residents and tourists in celebration of Songkran, the official start of the Buddhist New Year.

CAN DEAF PEOPLE COMMUNICATE WHILE ASLEEP?

Yes. In a case study, a 71-year-old man used fluent sign language while he was fast asleep! Researchers were able to translate the signs and gain an idea of what he was dreaming about.

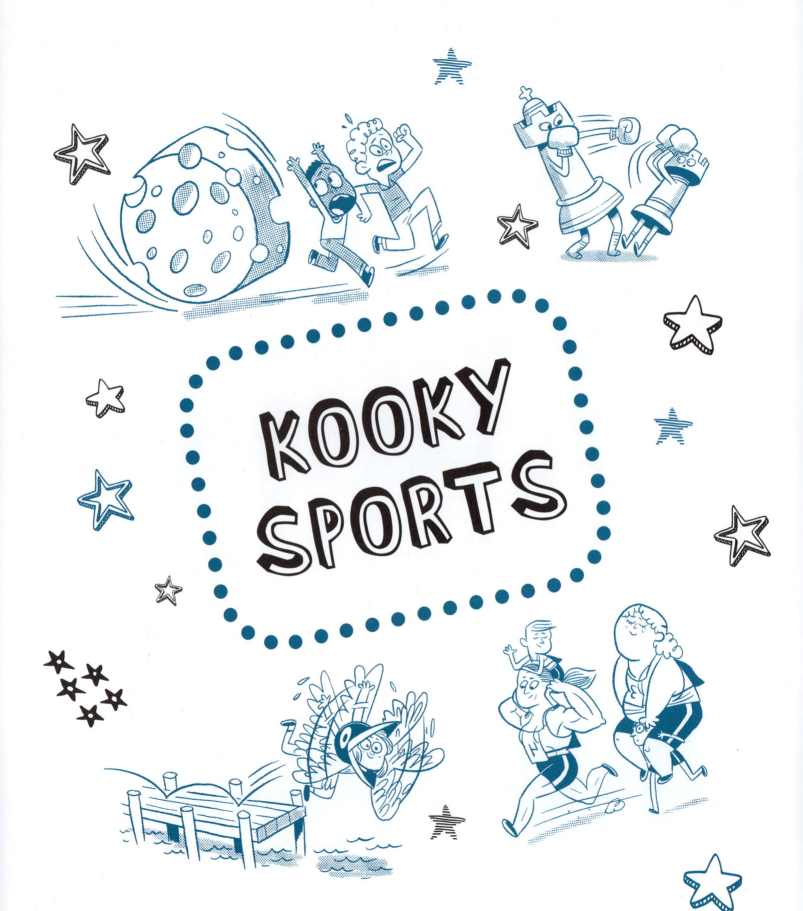

Kooky Sports

CAN YOU BECOME A LAWN MOWER-RACING CHAMP?

You may never get the chance to be a rally or Formula 1 driver, but how about lawn mower-racing champ? The British Lawn Mower Racing Association has four different classes for potential racers—from Class One's hand-pushed mowers to Class Four, which features wheel-based mowers that can achieve speeds of up to 80 km/h (50 mph). The annual 12-hour race sees up to three people per mower racing through the night around a track to see who can cover the 482 km (300 mi)-long distance the quickest!

DID YOU KNOW?

Canal jumping is a popular sport in the Netherlands. Contestants use a long pole positioned in the canal to help them leap across.

WHAT IS BOG SNORKELING?

During the month of August in the Waen Rhydd peat bog just outside Llanwrtyd Wells in Wales, two 55 m (180 ft)-long trenches are dug out for the annual bog-snorkeling competition. Contestants are required to swim down the trench wearing flippers and a snorkel, and whoever gets the quickest time is declared the winner.

WHAT'S WADING THROUGH A BOG LIKE?

Bog water has been described as having the consistency of pea soup. The smell is more than a bit stinky (and it tastes even worse), and if you're not wearing a wet suit, you can expect to find the water somewhat chilly. Tempted?

Kooky Sports

HOW OLD ARE THE OLDEST BODYBUILDERS?

American bodybuilder and yoga teacher Edith Connor clinched the record of oldest female bodybuilder in 2012 at the age of 77. She entered her first bodybuilding contest when she was 65—and came in first!

The oldest male bodybuilder is an American man named Jim Arrington, who entered the record books in 2015 aged 83.

HOW TALL CAN HUMAN TOWERS REACH?

The tallest *castell* ever made had nine levels and reached 12 m (39 ft). Children are often used for the top level because they're light and agile.

WHERE DO PEOPLE STAND ON TOP OF ONE ANOTHER?

The biannual Castells Competition, held in Tarragona in the south of Spain, sees teams of competitors called *colles* gather together in the city's bullring to build the highest human tower. The tower is started by strong *castellers* at the bottom, who are surrounded and supported by a mass of people acting as the foundations.

Then, there is a rush as the rest of the *castellers* leap into action, stepping onto each other's shoulders, forming the tower as quickly and carefully as possible. The towers can end up with 10 levels of *castellers* on top of each other!

Kooky Sports

CAN YOU OUTRUN A CHEESE?

The world's strangest cheese event may be the one at Cooper's Hill in Gloucestershire, UK. Every year, crowds amass to watch folk from all over the world take part in the infamous cheese-rolling event. There are five races. For each round, up to 20 people get ready at the top of a steep hill before a large cheese round begins rolling down the hill. The competitors then have to chase it down the 183 m (600 ft)-long, near-vertical slope. Whoever reaches the bottom first is declared the winner. The circular cheese reaches speeds up to 112 km/h (70 mph) and takes just 12 seconds to reach the bottom.

DID YOU KNOW?

Alan "Nasty" Nash of Britain has won the toe wrestling World Championships a record 16 times.

WHERE DO THEY CELEBRATE VIKING RAIDS?

The Scottish Shetland Islands celebrate the arrival of the Vikings over 1,000 years ago with the annual Up Helly Aa festival in January. The main event involves a squad of men dressed up as Vikings marching through the streets of Lerwick, dragging a 9 m (30 ft)-long replica of a Viking galley. They're followed by over 900 *guisers*—folk dressed in disguises. Once the procession reaches its end, the boat is set on fire amid music and fireworks. The festival boasts of being the biggest fire festival in Europe.

Kooky Sports

CAN YOU BUNGEE JUMP WITH A CROWD?

Yes, though it doesn't look comfortable. A mixed group of 25 jumpers attempted the trick from a platform suspended in front of the twin towers of the Deutsche Bank headquarters in Germany. The jump saw the tightly packed-together group plummeting 52 m (171 ft) before bouncing back up.

WHO RACES WITH HIS WIFE ON HIS BACK?

The sport may have started out as a joke back in 1992, but the Finnish Wife Carrying Championships are now a worldwide phenomenon, with competitions taking place in the USA, China, Britain, Italy, and Australia. The race involves a contestant carrying his wife over his shoulders as he runs along a 253 m (830 ft)-long assault course, including through water. The champion receives the equivalent of his wife's weight in beer as a prize.

CAN YOU PLAY GOLF ON A PLANE?

While you might be told off for rehearsing your golf swing in flight, there is a place you can whack a golf ball on the outside of a plane. The Swing on the Wing contest, held in Abu Dhabi, United Arab Emirates, sees pro and amateur golf players stand on a parked Airbus A340 wing and try and hit the ball as far as they can.

Kooky Sports

HOW CAN YOU MAKE A MARATHON MORE INTERESTING?

In Llanwrtyd Wells, Wales, the town's residents dreamt up a way of making marathons more interesting by having humans race against horses over a 35 km (22 mi)-long moorland course. It shouldn't come as a huge surprise to learn that the horses took the top prize almost every time. That was until the 25th anniversary of the event, when Huw Lobb beat the fastest horse by two minutes. By that time, annual prize money had accumulated over 25 years, leaving Lobb with a handsome cheque for £25,000 (about $32,000)!

WHEN DID THE FIRST OFFICIAL MARATHON HAPPEN?

The first modern marathon was held at the 1896 Olympic Games in Athens. The winner was a Greek man named Spyridon Louis, who did it in just under three hours.

DID YOU KNOW?

American Dale Webster surfed every day between September 2, 1975, and February 29, 2004, clocking up a record 14,641 consecutive days of surfing.

WHAT DO YOU GET IF YOU CROSS CHESS WITH BOXING?

The two sports seem badly matched, but that hasn't stopped the Chess Boxing World Championship from mixing the two. Chess boxing sees two brainy fighters alternating between punching each other, then sitting down in the middle of the ring for a game of chess. There are a total of 11 rounds, unless there is a knockout or a checkmate: six rounds of chess in four-minute rounds and five rounds of fisticuffs that last three minutes each.

Kooky Sports

IS THERE AN UNDERWATER OLYMPIC GAMES?

While the Olympic Games were taking place in Beijing, China, in 2008, Qiandao Underwater World in China decided to host their own events underwater. Laden in wet suits and scuba gear, divers undertook a host of events, including fencing, ring tossing, gymnastics, hurdles, and shooting. Divers who took part in the shooting event had to stand on a metal wire before trying to hit the target—an inflated balloon placed 5 m (16 ft) away from them. Spectators could watch from behind a large glass wall.

DID UNDERWATER SPORTS TAKE OFF?

Other countries that also got involved with the underwater sport craze include South Korea, where the Coex Aquarium ran events, including underwater soccer, weight lifting, Tae Kwon Do, and even grass hockey. Amazingly, play wasn't called off due to a waterlogged field.

DID YOU KNOW?

Early ice hockey pucks were made from frozen cow poop ... And the first golf balls had a core made from feathers, while the outer layer was made from leather.

DID YOU KNOW?

There are golf balls on the Moon. They were left there by US astronaut Alan Shepard, commander of NASA's Apollo 14 mission in 1971. He used a golf club made from a rock-sample scoop to hit them, under the Moon's low gravity.

Kooky Sports

HOW DO YOU PLAY SPORTS WITHOUT RULES?

The annual Shrovetide football match, held in Ashbourne, UK, is known as "no rules" soccer. The premise is simple—two teams made up of opposing people from opposite ends of the town play a game where the respective goals are 5 km (3 mi) apart. The game boasts hundreds of players and is played over two days, with each half lasting a wearisome eight hours!

DID YOU KNOW?

A golf ball has around 400 dimples on it. The dimples make the ball travel farther.

ARE THERE REALLY NO RULES?

Well, actually, there is one ancient rule in Shrovetide that demands that nobody may murder anyone during the course of the match. The batty soccer game is believed to be up to 1,000 years old and some think that in olden times, a severed head fresh from an execution was used to play the game instead of a football …

WHO PLAYS GOLF WITH POOP?

The annual Cow Dung Golf Tournament sees competitors marching up the Swiss Alps where cattle roam free, before seeing who can hit the most piles of cow poop within a two-hour period. Normal golf clubs are used during this 120-minute poop fest, and one can only imagine the mess you and your golf gear are left in once the dung has settled.

Kooky Sports

DID YOU KNOW?

The first organized college American football game took place in 1869. The two sides were Rutgers University and the College of New Jersey (now known as Princeton University).

WHAT IS THE WORLD'S FANCIEST GAME?

To qualify to play the Eton Wall Game, you first have to get into the UK's famous Eton College and then have parents with deep enough pockets to pay the fees for it. Past pupils have included prime ministers and princes. The game features two teams who must battle it out to get a ball from one end of a wall to the other using their feet. The outcome is usually goalless, because students simply pile up against the wall and dive into anyone unfortunate enough to have the ball in their possession. Rules include no "furking," "sneaking," or "knuckling"—whatever that is.

HOW DANGEROUS IS AMERICAN FOOTBALL?

You took your life into your hands playing American football in its early years. In the 1905 season, 18 players were killed, and more than 150 were seriously injured.

DID YOU KNOW?

The balls used in American football are not made from pigskin and likely never have been. The inside of the ball may once have been made from an inflated pig's bladder, but these days the inside is made from rubber and the outside is made from cowhide.

Kooky Sports

WHAT IS HORNUSSEN?

It's difficult to describe the Swiss sport of hornussen, other than that it looks ridiculous. A player thwacks a small, rubber puck called a "hornuss," mounted on a launcher, with a 2 m (6.5 ft)-long, fishing-rod-style flexible club. The hornuss whizzes through the air at up to 320 km/h (199 mph) toward the opposing team of up to 18 players, who are all lined up in a field and holding wooden placards used to catch the hornuss. The team win points for catching the puck. There are over 200 clubs and 8,500 players dedicated to the sport of hornussen.

CAN YOU WIN BIG MONEY PLAYING ROCK, PAPER, SCISSORS?

While you might think of rock, paper, scissors as a schoolyard game, it is actually a full-blown professional sport with a top prize of £36,190 (about $46,420) up for grabs. The prize is offered at the televized USA Rock Paper Scissors League Tournament.

DID YOU KNOW?

Rock, paper, scissors is thought to be the oldest hand game in the world. It may have originated in China more than 2,000 years ago.

IS THERE A MORE DANGEROUS VERSION OF ROCK, PAPER, SCISSORS?

Some players don't simply stick with rock, paper, and scissors—they have also been known to introduce "trump" moves such as dynamite. However, there is some dispute over whether dynamite would actually win, because some believe paper would in fact beat a stick of dynamite because it would smother its wick. There's also a version that features 22 different objects, including guns, lightning, axes, fire, snakes, and nuclear weapons!

Kooky Sports

DID YOU KNOW?

As a unique take on the sport of polo, some people choose to play the game while riding unicycles rather than the more traditional horses.

WHAT IS EXTREME IRONING?

Extreme ironing is a way to add thrills to getting rid of creases. Ironing clothes is a dull task at the best of times, but what if you tried it while hanging off the side of a cliff? The Extreme Ironing World Championship, held in Germany, has competitors, irons, and ironing boards set up in bizarre locations. These have included climbing a wall while pressing clothes and ironing while halfway up a tree.

IS SHIN-KICKING A SPORT?

Shin-kicking is a combat sport that is thought to have originated in the 17th Century in England and is still played today. The aim of the game is to kick your opponent's shins, while avoiding being kicked yourself. Contestants wear special padding, and there are strict rules, so don't go trying this out on your friends and family!

WHAT HAPPENS IN THE REDNECK GAMES?

The Redneck Games in East Dublin, Georgia, USA, started in 1996 as a small event to gently mock the Olympic Games being held in Atlanta up the road. They are now a national institution attracting thousands of people. Crazy events include bobbing for pigs' feet, making fart noises with your armpit, the mud-pit belly flop, toilet seat tossing, seed spitting, and comparing butts! The prize for most events is a trophy with a crushed beer can on top.

Kooky Sports

DOES DOING PUZZLES BURN CALORIES?

Your brain burns a lot of calories—about 400-500 per day—and that's just when it is carrying out everyday functions. Some studies have suggested that it burns even more calories when it is required to tackle tricky problems, such as solving puzzles or concentrating in class. No wonder you're so hungry when you get home from school!

CAN YOU FLY WITHOUT A PLANE?

In the UK seaside town of Bognor Regis each year, people threw themselves off a pier using bizarre homemade flying contraptions. Many were plain ridiculous and designed to make spectators laugh as competitors plunged into the sea from a great height. Competitors dressed as the Pope, Donald Duck, Doctor Who (with TARDIS), Ninja Turtles, Wonder Woman, and a chicken and mushroom pie. Other, more committed engineers built gliders to try to reach some distance. If anyone managed to fly 100 m (328 ft), they were awarded £25,000 (about $32,000). Sadly, the competition stopped in 2016, though some hope it may happen again in the future.

WHAT'S THE LONGEST SOMEONE HAS STAYED AWAKE WITHOUT HELP?

The official record number of hours a person has stayed awake without the use of stimulants is 264 hours, which is just over 11 days! The record was set under test conditions in 1965 by a high school student named Randy Gardner.

DID YOU KNOW?

Each May, there is a world paper airplane championship. Held in the USA, contestants travel from around the world to try their hand in several categories.

PREPOSTEROUS PASTIMES

Preposterous Pastimes

DID YOU KNOW?

It's impossible to tickle yourself. Go on—try it!

HOW CAN YOU BECOME A STAR WARS STORM TROOPER?

The 501st Legion is Earth's biggest group of organized Star Wars fans, and they love to dress up in homemade storm trooper costumes. The Force is strong in this group, because they have more than 14,000 members from over 30 countries. And the good news is that, as long as you have a proper storm trooper costume and are over the age of 18, you can sign up for the 501st Legion today!

CAN YOU TRAIN TO BE A JEDI?

While you might not get to wield the Force like a Jedi Knight from the Star Wars movies, you can train to use a lightsaber. Ludosport Lightsaber Combat Academy in Milan, Italy, offers fans lessons in seven styles of Jedi combat. As well as lightsaber skills, you can learn how to stop Darth Maul with a throw and whip Darth Vader's lightsaber out of his clutches!

167

Preposterous Pastimes

DO YOU NEED LESSONS IN LAUGHING?

World Laughter Day is an event designed to giggle away your blues. Laughter can lower stress and anxiety levels and even strengthen your immune system. The "Guru of Giggling," Dr. Madan Kataria, created Laughter Yoga in order to teach people the principles of laughter therapy in over 60 countries—and there are now over 20,000 Laughter Yoga clubs all over the planet.

DID YOU KNOW?

Competitive duck herding is a sport in some places. Dogs are trained to herd ducks and show off their skills in competitions.

WHOSE BARBECUE WAS THE BIGGEST?

The people of Mexico organized a record-shattering barbecue in Monterrey, Nuevo Leon. An amazing 45,252 people attended—that's a lot of burgers!

WHAT'S THE RECORD FOR MAKING SNOW ANGELS?

Lying on the snow and waving your arms and legs to leave the impression of an angel is fun. Now imagine sharing the experience with over 8,962 other folk in winter wear. The city of Bismarck, North Dakota, USA, invited residents to the state capitol grounds in February 2007 for the record-setting event. Everyone got involved—the youngest snow angel was six-week-old baby Jack Deitz, and the oldest participant was 99-year-old Pauline Jaeger.

Preposterous Pastimes

CAN YOU BALLROOM DANCE UNDERWATER?

Seventy-four Australian scuba divers set a world record for ballroom dancing underwater, with a class at Sydney's Olympic Park Aquatic Centre. The entire dancing sequence lasted for 13 minutes and 30 seconds. If the idea of scuba ballroom dancing doesn't appeal, you can always try underwater ballet, as Olympic medal-winning Miho Takeda did in Tokyo in 2008.

HOW MANY SKYDIVERS CAN JUMP IN FORMATION?

Flying in formation with just a few skydivers takes skill, training, and a lot of patience. So getting 68 skydivers to break the largest wingsuit formation record over Lake Elsinore in California was no mean feat. It took five days of solid practice to beat the world record, with the team jumping an incredible 30 times before deciding that they were ready for an official try. Four planes were used, each carrying a team of skydivers who leapt out and then fell at vertical speeds of 109 km/h (67 mph) to reach a V formation. There was only 3 m (10 ft) separating them when they released their parachutes.

CAN YOU GRAFFITI OBJECTS USING YARN?

Yes! Yarn bombing is when people use knitted or crotcheted yarn to decorate objects in the street.

DID YOU KNOW?

The deepest half-marathon took place in a Polish salt mine at a depth of 212 m (695 ft).

Preposterous Pastimes

DID YOU KNOW?
A Serbian soccer player who was dropped from his club got his own back by churning up the field with a tractor.

WHERE DO VIDEO GAME CHARACTERS HANG OUT?
In 2008, a group of video game fans gathered on London's Millennium Bridge in an attempt to break the world record for most video game characters in one place. Though only 80 characters showed up, they still managed to shatter the record—because they were the first to try!

WHO PLAYED THE LONGEST GAME OF TELEPHONE?
In a game of telephone, a player whispers a message to the person next to them, and the phrase is passed down the line to see if it comes out the same at the end. It rarely does! In the longest game of telephone, 1,792 people gathered in Tauranga, New Zealand, to support Hearing Awareness Week. The message started as "turn it down," and eventually turned into "Tauranga schools." Not a bad effort!

WOULD YOU TAKE A TRAIN IN YOUR UNDERWEAR?
In November 2008, commuters at London St. Pancras train station in the UK were confronted by 116 people dressed in just their underwear in an attempt to say "Pants To Poverty," promoting fair-trade products and rights. All the participants received a free pair of underwear.

Preposterous Pastimes

WHO IS THE WORLD'S ODDEST PROTESTER?

Protester and a performance artist Mark McGowan knows how to get attention for his causes. He sat in a tub of baked beans for two weeks to support the British fried breakfast, and tried to cartwheel from Brighton to London with two rocks strapped to his feet to protest against people taking pebbles from Brighton's beach. (He ended up in the hospital.) Mark's attempt to "sail" from London to Glasgow in a shopping cart to improve relations between England and Scotland sadly failed. He only managed to complete 105 km (65 mi) of the 644 km (400 mi)-long journey due to adverse weather conditions.

CAN YOU POWER A LIGHT BULB WITH YOUR HEAD?

Retired highway-maintenance engineer Zhang Deke from Altay, China, liked to charge himself with 220 volts of electricity as part of his exercise routine, which left his body "charged." He could then place light bulbs on his head and ears and actually light them. Zhang was also able to cook a fish on his belly in two minutes with the powers of his electrically charged body.

CAN YOU RACE IN HIGH-HEELED SHOES?

It's possible, but not easy. Just ask the 967 men and women who gathered in Fort Wayne, Indiana, USA, to race in high heels to raise money for charity. Every participant was fitted with a pair of bright red stiletto heels, and they ran—or stumbled—around the 100 m (330 ft)-long course, blowing the previous record of 763 racers out of the water.

Preposterous Pastimes

SHOULD YOU EAT ON THE TOILET?

The Modern Toilet diner in Taipei was flush with ideas for dining gimmicks. Its seats were converted toilet bowls and one of the most popular dishes was ice cream in the shape of dog poop. It was so popular, it led to another 11 branches opening.

WHERE DO DOCTORS PRESCRIBE DINNER?

Also in Taipei, the DS Music restaurant provided dinner served by doctors and nurses while water came from IV drips mounted in the ceiling. The toilet in the hospital restaurant was named the Emergency Room. How very apt!

WHAT IS THE SMARTEST ROBOT IN THE WORLD?

A robot named Sophia, created in 2016, was once deemed to be the smartest robot in the world. Sophia, who was developed by Hanson Robotics in Hong Kong, China, can understand human speech, hold conversations, and even recognize individuals. She was named the United Nations Development Program's Innovation Champion, making her the first ever nonhuman to be given a title by the United Nations.

CAN YOU RENT A ROOM IN PRISON?

The Alcatraz Hotel is a converted prison in the German city of Kaiserslautern. If it sounds like your thing, you can spend the evening in one of its 57 "cells." You'll sleep on an original prison bed in a traditional convict uniform, next to a toilet behind a heavy steel door and barred windows.

Preposterous Pastimes

DID YOU KNOW?
There are loads of different types of eating competitions. One involves contestants eating as many stinging nettles as possible in one minute, while in another, people are timed to see how fast they can eat an entire pizza.

WHAT IS THE MOST DANGEROUS DINNER?

Japanese diners enjoy the dangerous delicacy Fugu globefish. A deadly toxin can be found throughout the fish's body—in its organs, membrane, and even its skin. To be able to eat the fish and survive requires the skills of a specialist licensed chef. It costs up to 20,000 yen (about £100/$130) to enjoy the thrill.

HOW DO YOU COOK THE PERFECT SPIDER FEAST?

To cook the perfect spider, pan fry it with salt and garlic. When its skin has gone deep red-brown, eat it hot—ideally, the fried spider should be crisp on the outside but juicy on the inside. Bon appétit!

WHERE CAN YOU EAT CRISPY FRIED SPIDERS?

Spiders are a huge seller in Cambodia, where they are regarded as a delicacy. The spiders, which breed in holes in the ground, look similar to tarantulas and are fried in woks at local markets. Although poisonous when alive, the spider's venom is rendered harmless once cooked, and eating the eight-legged critter is supposed to have medicinal benefits, too—Cambodians say that it can help with coughs, backache, and breathing problems.

Preposterous Pastimes

WOULD YOU KISS A VENOMOUS SNAKE?

Brave snake charmer Khum Chaibuddee attempted to break the world record for the most venomous snakes ever kissed. His Thai audience must have held their collective breaths as 19 king cobras slithered their way onstage to be confronted by Khum, with his puckered-up lips at the ready. There is no word on whether or not Khum took any of the snakes out on a date after.

CAN YOU GO TO CIRCUS SCHOOL?

If you want a truly unique education, enroll at the Coney Island Sideshow School in Brooklyn, New York, USA. Here, you can be taught how to be a circus performer in seven days. That means learning the art of sword swallowing, glass walking, lying on a bed of nails, breathing fire, and escaping from a straitjacket while hanging upside down.

WHERE CAN YOU BE MASSAGED BY SNAKES?

At an event in the Philippines, brave spectators could be massaged by four enormous pythons with a combined weight of 250 kg (550 lb).

WHAT FURRY FAST FOOD MIGHT YOU FIND IN MALAWI?

If you should find yourself driving down the roads of Malawi, why not pull over and enjoy the local delicacy of mouse-on-a-stick? For a bargain price, you can buy a dried-out mouse as a tasty example of African fast food. The head, skin, bones, and intestines are all included in the price!

Preposterous Pastimes

WHOSE FACE BECAME A HOME FOR SNAILS?

At the age of nine, schoolgirl Tiana Walton set a world record for having the most snails sliming their way all over her face—25 of them! The rules for setting the record were strict but simple—Tiana had to put as many snails as possible on her face in one minute. Once done, she then had to tip her head forward—any snails that fell off over a 10-second period were disallowed.

WHO IS THE SCORPION QUEEN?

Malaysian bug enthusiast Nur Malena Hassan earned the title of "Scorpion Queen" after spending 36 days in a glass cage with 6,069 venomous scorpions. She was stung 17 times during her time with the arachnids, but had spent several years building up an immunity to scorpion poison, so luckily she survived!

WHERE MIGHT YOU FIND A 20-TON SPIDER?

French company La Machine built a 15 m (49 ft) high giant robotic spider named La Princesse to wow crowds. It takes 12 people strapped inside to control the spider's 50 axes of movement and mimic creepy-crawly motions. They can also control jets of water, which shoot out of La Princesse's abdomen.

WHO CRIES MILKY TEARS?

While swimming, Turkish construction worker Ilker Yilmaz discovered that he could squirt water out of his eye. After that, he decided to find out just what else he could squirt out and over what distance. At a public event in Istanbul, Ilker grossed out his audience by snorting milk up his nose, then shooting out a 2.8 m (9.1 ft)-long squirt of milk from his left eye. He also managed to put out five lit candles in over two minutes using his amazing milk-shooting ability.

175

Preposterous Pastimes

HOW MANY LIVE BEES CAN YOU HOLD IN YOUR MOUTH AT ONE TIME?

Playing the clarinet while covered in bees is just one of Norman Gary's amazing tricks. He has also appeared on more than 70 television shows, done six commercials featuring bees, and has also been a bee "wrangler" for 18 movies—meaning that he trains and takes care of bees when they are needed in front of the cameras. On top of all that, he set a world record when he held 109 bees in his closed mouth for 10 seconds while they feasted on a sugar syrup-soaked sponge!

WHERE IS THE SAFEST PLACE TO BE AN ANT?

Buddhist monks refuse to kill any of the ants infesting their Kuala Lumpur temple because of their beliefs in nonviolence ... even when one monk was hospitalized with ant bites!

WHO HAS THE BIGGEST COLLECTION OF GUM WRAPPERS?

American Gary Duschl has been collecting gum wrappers for more than 60 years. He links these in a record-breaking gum wrapper chain that currently contains nearly 3 million wrappers and is 36,800 m (120,750 ft) long!

WHO HOLDS THE RECORD FOR HAVING THE MOST INSECT TATTOOS?

Michael Amoia from the USA broke the world record for the greatest number insect tattoos in 2021 with an astonishing 864. His next nearest rival at the time was Baxter Milsom from the UK, who had a paltry 402. Baxter's tattoos depict a complete A–Z of insects, from alligator bugs to zebra swallowtail butterflies.